◆ THE FLAVORS OF ◆
BON APPÉTIT

• THE FLAVORS OF •

BON APPÉTIT

• 1994 •

from the Editors of Bon Appétit

Condé Nast Books ◆ Pantheon
New York

For *Condé Nast* Books

Jill Cohen, *Vice President*
Ellen Maria Bruzelius, *Direct Marketing Director*
Kristine Smith-Cunningham, *Advertising Promotion Manager*
Lisa Faith Phillips, *Fulfillment Manager*
Tina Kessler, *Direct Marketing Administrator*
Jennifer Metz, *Direct Marketing Associate*

For *Bon Appétit* Magazine

Laurie Glenn Buckle
Marcy MacDonald
William J. Garry
Barbara Fairchild
John Hartung
Devon Holmes
Marcia Lewis
Lisa Rose

Produced by Joshua Morris Publishing, Inc.,
221 Danbury Road, Wilton, Connecticut 06897.

Designed by Laura Hammond Hough.

Olivada Crostini, page 14, and Orecchiette Pasta with Peas and Onions, page 110,
Copyright © 1994 by Vegetable Kingdom, Inc. Reprinted by permission of
Simon & Schuster, Inc.

Front Jacket: Almond Cheesecake Fruit Tart (page 169).

Back Jacket: Tomato, Cheese and Herb Tart (page 20); Spicy Tofu and Vegetable Stir-fry
with Soba Noodles (page 102); Top Sirloin Steak with Bell Pepper and Onion Sauté
(page 49).

Page 5: Mixed Berry Tiramisù (page 195); Lamb Fillet with Thai Curry Sauce (page 57);
Goat Cheese Dip with Crudités (page 17).

Library of Congress Cataloging-in-Publication Data

The Flavors of Bon Appétit / by the editors of Bon Appétit.
    p.   cm.
    ISBN 0-679-43960-9
    1. Cookery.   I. Bon Appétit.
TX714.F69   1994
641.5--dc 20   94-13381
                                                                      CIP

Manufactured in Italy
FIRST EDITION
2 4 6 8 9 7 5 3 1

◆ Contents ◆

◆Introduction◆

Certain recipes live on long after they appear in the pages of *Bon Appétit*. They are the ones that we, the magazine's editors, add to our personal recipe files for reasons many and varied. In other words, they are our favorites.

For this spectacular new book, we have opened up those files and selected what were among the best recipes of the many hundreds we ran in 1993. There are more than 200 of them here, from appetizers right through desserts, covering every type of dish as surely as they cover the globe. There are simple foods, easy-to-make and quick-to-cook dishes, and there are sophisticated recipes, perfect for pulling out all the stops on a special occasion. There are also recipes for those who keep to a health-conscious diet, in and among some of the kind of indulgences we all deserve.

We like to think you will find your favorites here, too.

Clockwise from far left: Artichoke and Fennel Ravioli with Tomato-Fennel Sauce, page 112; Spinach with Olives, Raisins and Pine Nuts, page 126; Mashed Potatoes and Butternut Squash, page 130; Roast Veal Brisket with Marsala-Mushroom Sauce, page 53.

◆ Starters ◆

There are any number of ways to begin a meal: with an elegant, artfully composed appetizer; with a warming bowl of soup; with an exotic drink; with simple, tasty finger foods. You'll find them all here, and then some. Whether you're planning a formal affair around the dining room table or something casual in front of the television, look to this chapter for the starter that best suits the occasion.

If it's dinner in the kitchen with friends, try the savory Roasted Garlic and Brie Toasts (page 14), while the Fontina, Corn and Jalapeño Quesadillas (page 22) would make a fine beginning to a fireside chili supper. Get Sunday brunch off to a lively start with Cranberry Rose Punch (page 39), or offer the lovely Fennel, Apple and Almond Soup (page 31) as a prelude to a late-night menu. But these are just suggestions; let your imagination guide you through the possibilities.

Mini Chicken Tostadas, page 12.

When setting the table, there's no need to follow the old rules anymore. Take a look at the serving pieces and accessories you already own, then dream up different ways to use them.

Here are some easy ideas to try, but don't limit yourself to only these possibilities. They're just a little inspiration for creating settings of your own design.

Glass Acts

Margarita glasses are good for something other than that popular tequila cocktail. They're the perfect shape and size for fresh fruit compotes. Dip the rim of the glass in lime juice and brown sugar, and then fill with a mixture of seasonal fruits. Top with a squeeze of lime juice and a splash of Cointreau.

◆ ◆ ◆

◆ APPETIZERS ◆

Tricolor Vegetable Pâté

◆ ◆ ◆

2   *15-ounce cans cannellini (white kidney beans), rinsed, drained thoroughly*
1   *tablespoon fresh lemon juice*
1   *tablespoon olive oil*
1   *tablespoon minced fresh oregano or 1 teaspoon dried*
2   *garlic cloves, pressed*

1   *7-ounce jar roasted red bell peppers, drained, chopped*
3/4 *cup crumbled feta cheese (about 4 ounces)*

2   *garlic cloves*
1   *cup fresh basil leaves*
1   *cup fresh Italian parsley leaves*
1/4 *cup toasted pine nuts*
3   *tablespoons olive oil*
1/2 *cup low-fat ricotta cheese*

Fresh herb sprigs
Sourdough bread slices or breadsticks

Line 8½ x 4½-inch loaf pan with plastic, overlapping sides.

FOR BEAN LAYER: Mash beans in large bowl. Add lemon juice, 1 tablespoon olive oil, oregano and 2 garlic cloves and blend until smooth. Season to taste with salt and pepper. Spread bean mixture evenly on bottom of prepared pan.

FOR RED PEPPER LAYER: Combine peppers and feta in processor and blend until smooth. Spread pepper mixture evenly over bean layer in prepared dish.

FOR PESTO LAYER: Mince 2 garlic cloves in processor. Add basil, parsley and pine nuts and mince. With machine running, gradually add 3 tablespoons oil through feed tube and process until smooth. Mix in ricotta. Spread pesto evenly over red pepper layer. Cover with plastic wrap and refrigerate overnight.

To unmold, invert pâté onto serving platter. Peel off plastic wrap from pâté. Garnish with herb sprigs and serve with sourdough bread slices or breadsticks.

12 TO 14 SERVINGS

Scallops Baked in Phyllo with Lemon Butter

◆ ◆ ◆

1   tablespoon butter
2   tablespoons minced shallot
½   cup dry white wine
2   tablespoons whipping cream

6   phyllo pastry sheets
½   cup (1 stick) butter, melted
8   large sea scallops
1   tablespoon brandy (optional)
1   teaspoon minced fresh marjoram or ¼ teaspoon dried

1   large egg yolk
5   tablespoons butter
1½ tablespoons fresh lemon juice

FOR SAUCE: Melt 1 tablespoon butter in heavy small saucepan over medium heat. Add shallot and sauté 3 minutes. Add wine and boil until liquid is reduced to ¼ cup, 5 minutes. Mix in cream.

FOR SCALLOPS: Place 1 phyllo sheet on work surface (keep remaining phyllo covered). Brush with melted butter. Top with second sheet. Brush with melted butter. Top with third sheet. Brush with butter. Cut phyllo stack into four 6-inch squares. Place 1 scallop in center of each square. Brush scallops with brandy and sprinkle with marjoram. Season with salt and pepper. Pull up all sides of phyllo around scallops, forming pouches. Pinch center to seal. Repeat process with remaining 3 phyllo sheets, melted butter, scallops, brandy and marjoram. Arrange pouches on baking sheet. Brush with melted butter. *(Sauce and pouches can be made 4 hours ahead. Cover separately and chill.)*

Preheat oven to 425°F. Bake pastry pouches until golden, approximately 10 minutes.

Meanwhile, rewarm sauce over medium-low heat. Whisk in yolk; do not boil. Add 5 tablespoons butter and whisk just until melted. Add lemon juice and season with salt and pepper. Spoon sauce onto 4 plates. Top each with 2 pastry pouches.

4 SERVINGS

Pitcher This

Don't believe them when they tell you bread has to be served in a basket. Breadsticks are right at home in an earthenware pitcher. Sweet butter packed in a small wooden dough bowl adds to the warm country look.

Flowers by the Jar

For an informal table, wildflowers are better suited to homey canning jars than fancy vases. Tinted jars add a hint of color; they're widely available at flea markets and tag sales across the country.

◆ ◆ ◆

DOING DIM SUM

For the Chinese, dim sum is more than a meal: it is a cultural happening. Credited to the tenth-century Cantonese, dim sum is linked to the tradition of drinking tea. From early morning to mid-afternoon, the Chinese teahouse, like the Western coffee shop, was where people came to talk business and gossip.

The typical dim sum lunch includes everything from pancakes, rolls, buns, balls and dumplings to soups, tarts and cakes. It's definitely a meal to savor at a restaurant, since there are far too many dishes to make at home. And some of the best dim sum restaurants are, as you might imagine, in Hong Kong.

◆ ◆ ◆

Mini Chicken Tostadas

◆ ◆ ◆

9   6-inch corn tortillas
    Vegetable oil

¼   cup olive oil
½   cup matchstick-size strips red onion
½   cup matchstick-size strips red bell pepper
½   cup matchstick-size strips carrot
2   large garlic cloves, chopped
2   tablespoons tomato sauce
2   tablespoons chicken broth
1   teaspoon ground cumin
1   cup diced cooked chicken

1½ cups Black Beans with Tomato and Bell Pepper
    (see recipe below)

Using 3-inch round cookie cutter, cut out 2 rounds from each tortilla. Pour vegetable oil into large skillet to depth of ½ inch. Heat over medium-high heat until hot. Add tortillas in batches and fry until crisp, turning once, about 1 minute. Drain on paper towels.

Heat olive oil in heavy large skillet over medium heat. Add onion, bell pepper, carrot and garlic and sauté 2 minutes. Add tomato sauce, broth and cumin and simmer until thickened, about 3 minutes. Mix in chicken.

Preheat oven to 350°F. Place tortillas on cookie sheet. Top each with generous tablespoon black beans, then chicken mixture. Bake until heated through, about 15 minutes.

MAKES 18

Black Beans with Tomato and Bell Pepper

5   cups dried black beans

12 cups water
1   small red onion, chopped
1   green bell pepper, chopped
3   large bay leaves

½   cup olive oil
4   cups chopped tomatoes
1   small onion, chopped
1   fresh cilantro bunch, chopped

¹/₄ cup chopped garlic

1 tablespoon ground cumin

Place beans in large pot with enough cold water to cover by 3 inches. Soak overnight. Drain.

Return beans to pot. Add 12 cups water, red onion, bell pepper and bay leaves and bring to boil. Reduce heat to medium and cook until beans are tender, stirring occasionally, about 1¹/₂ hours. Drain. Transfer to bowl.

Heat oil in pot over medium heat. Add remaining ingredients; sauté 2 minutes. Add beans; stir to heat through.

MAKES ABOUT 8 CUPS

Chicken Liver and Red Pepper Spiedini

◆ ◆ ◆

¹/₂ cup olive oil

2 tablespoons chopped fresh rosemary or 1 tablespoon dried

2 tablespoons minced fresh garlic

2 tablespoons white wine vinegar

1 tablespoon minced lemon peel (yellow part only)

12 chicken livers (about 1 pound), trimmed, halved

32 1¹/₂-inch red bell pepper squares (from about 2 bell peppers)

8 bamboo skewers, soaked in water 30 minutes

4 6-inch pieces French bread baguette, halved lengthwise

Fresh rosemary sprigs (optional)

Whisk first 5 ingredients in medium bowl to blend; season dressing to taste with salt and pepper. Transfer half of dressing to small bowl and reserve. Add chicken livers and pepper squares to dressing in medium bowl. Toss to coat well. Marinate 1 hour at room temperature. (Can be prepared 1 day ahead. Cover liver mixture and reserved dressing separately and refrigerate.)

Preheat oven to 400°F. Alternate 4 pepper squares and 3 liver pieces on each skewer. Arrange on baking sheet. Place bread, cut side up, on same sheet. Brush bread with some reserved dressing. Bake skewers and bread 6 minutes. Turn skewers over and bake skewers and bread until livers are cooked through, 8 minutes longer.

Place 1 toast on each plate. Place 1 skewer atop each toast. Brush lightly with remaining dressing. Garnish with rosemary.

8 SERVINGS

◆ ◆ ◆

In Italy, *spiedini* are skewers of any combination of foods — bread, cheeses, meatballs, fish — that can be grilled or roasted. To complete this elegant appetizer, serve them with a bottle of Asti Spumante, the Italian sparkling wine.

◆ ◆ ◆

Roasted Garlic and Brie Toasts

◆ ◆ ◆

24 thin French bread baguette slices
1½ tablespoons butter
1   large head garlic, cloves separated (unpeeled)
12 ounces ripe Brie cheese, rind removed, room temperature
     Pinch of cayenne pepper

     Chopped fresh arugula or watercress

Preheat oven to 350°F. Place baguette slices on cookie sheet. Bake until golden, about 10 minutes. Cool. Melt butter in heavy small ovenproof skillet over medium heat. Add garlic and toss to coat. Transfer skillet to oven and bake garlic until knife pierces centers easily, about 20 minutes. Cool slightly. Peel garlic. Transfer garlic to bowl and mash with fork. Add Brie and cayenne and mix well. *(Can be made 6 hours ahead. Cover and let stand at room temperature.)*

Preheat broiler. Spread some cheese mixture on each toast (reserve remaining mixture for another use). Season with pepper. Broil until cheese bubbles. Sprinkle with chopped arugula. Transfer toasts to platter and serve.

6 SERVINGS

Here, slices of toasted French bread are spread with black olive paste (called *olivada*) and topped with roasted red bell peppers and cheese for an easy and impressive appetizer. For a mild-tasting olive paste, use pitted California ripe olives. If you prefer a more assertive flavor, use Mediterranean olives such as Kalamata or Niçoise.

◆ ◆ ◆

Olivada Crostini

◆ ◆ ◆

2 6-ounce cans pitted ripe whole medium olives, drained
3 tablespoons olive oil
2 tablespoons pine nuts, toasted
2 large garlic cloves

1 8-ounce French bread baguette, cut diagonally into slices

    Roasted red bell peppers (available in jars), sliced
    Mozzarella cheese, slivered

Blend first 4 ingredients in processor. Season olive paste to taste with salt and pepper. *(Can be made 1 week ahead. Cover and chill.)*

Preheat oven to 350°F. Place bread slices in single layer on baking sheet. Bake until lightly toasted, 10 minutes.

Spread olive paste on toasts. Top with bell peppers and cheese. Season with pepper and serve.

MAKES ABOUT 2 CUPS

Croutons with Smoked Salmon, Goat Cheese, Mustard and Dill

◆ ◆ ◆

2   *tablespoons honey mustard*
1   *tablespoon Dijon mustard*
1   *tablespoon finely chopped red onion*
1   *tablespoon drained capers*
2   *teaspoons minced fresh dill or $\frac{3}{4}$ teaspoon dillweed*
12   *$\frac{3}{8}$-inch-thick diagonally cut French bread baguette slices*
       Olive oil

4   *ounces soft mild goat cheese (such as Montrachet)*
3   *ounces thinly sliced smoked salmon*
       Fresh dill sprigs (optional)

Preheat oven to 350°F. Blend first 5 ingredients in small bowl. Arrange bread on baking sheet. Brush lightly with oil. Bake until crisp, about 10 minutes. Cool. *(Can be prepared up to 6 hours ahead. Cover mustard mixture and croutons separately; let stand at room temperature.)*

Spread croutons with goat cheese, then mustard mixture. Top with salmon. Garnish with dill, if desired.

MAKES 12

Wild Mushroom Timbales

◆ ◆ ◆

½   cup hot water
1   ounce dried porcini mushrooms
5   ounces fresh shiitake mushrooms

4   tablespoons (½ stick) butter
½   cup thinly sliced shallots
12 ounces button mushrooms, chopped
3   tablespoons dry white wine
1   cup chopped fresh parsley

1½ cups whipping cream
4   large eggs
2   large egg yolks
¼   teaspoon ground nutmeg

1   cup canned low-salt chicken broth
¼   cup whipping cream
6   tablespoons (¾ stick) butter
1   tablespoon minced fresh parsley

FOR TIMBALES: Combine ½ cup hot water and porcini mushrooms in bowl. Let mushrooms soak until soft, about 20 minutes. Strain porcini mushrooms and chop. Chop half of shiitake mushrooms; slice remaining shiitake mushrooms.

Melt 2 tablespoons butter in heavy large skillet over medium-high heat. Add shallots and sauté 3 minutes. Add button mushrooms. Cook until mushrooms are brown and dry, stirring occasionally, about 15 minutes. Add wine and boil 1 minute. Transfer mushrooms to medium bowl. Melt 1 tablespoon butter in same skillet over medium-low heat. Add porcini and chopped shiitake mushrooms. Cover and cook until tender, stirring occasionally, about 10 minutes. Add porcini mixture to button mushrooms in bowl. Stir in 1 cup parsley. Season with salt and pepper.

Melt 1 tablespoon butter in same skillet over medium heat. Add sliced shiitake mushrooms and sauté 5 minutes. Set shitake aside for garnish. *(Can be prepared 1 day ahead. Cover mushrooms separately and refrigerate.)*

Preheat oven to 350°F. Butter eight ¾-cup ramekins. Combine 1½ cups cream, eggs, egg yolks and nutmeg in large bowl. Season with salt and pepper. Place ⅓ cup mushroom mixture in each prepared ramekin. Pour ⅓ cup custard into each. Arrange ramekins in large roasting pan. Pour enough hot water into pan to come halfway up side of ramekins. Bake until custard is set, about 40 minutes.

MEANWHILE, PREPARE SAUCE: Boil broth and ¼ cup cream in heavy small saucepan until reduced to ⅓ cup, 15 minutes. Gradually whisk in 6 tablespoons butter. Stir in 1 tablespoon parsley. Season with salt and pepper.

Rewarm sliced shiitake mushrooms in heavy large skillet over medium heat. Run small sharp knife around sides of ramekins and invert timbales onto plates. Spoon sauce over and garnish with sliced shiitake mushrooms.

MAKES 8

Goat Cheese Dip with Crudités

◆ ◆ ◆

5 ½ ounces soft mild goat cheese (such as Montrachet)
2   tablespoons olive oil
3   tablespoons chopped radishes
2   tablespoons chopped green onion tops
½   pound green beans, trimmed

1   15-ounce can baby corn, drained
1   radish bunch, tops left on
      French bread baguette slices
      Additional chopped radishes
      Additional chopped green onion tops

Blend cheese, oil and generous amount of pepper in processor until smooth. Add 3 tablespoons chopped radishes and 2 tablespoons chopped green onion tops and just blend in. Transfer to bowl. Blanch green beans in large pot of boiling salted water until crisp-tender. Drain. Rinse with cold water. Drain well and pat dry. *(Goat cheese dip and beans can be prepared 1 day ahead. Cover separately and refrigerate.)*

Place dip in center of platter. Surround with green beans, corn, whole radishes and bread. Sprinkle dip with additional chopped radishes and onions.

4 SERVINGS

Lamb and Herbed Goat Cheese Bundles

◆ ◆ ◆

1   3.5-ounce log soft mild goat cheese (such as Montrachet)
1½ tablespoons finely chopped fresh sage leaves or ¾ teaspoon
    rubbed dried sage

1   5-pound leg of lamb, boned, butterflied, well trimmed
2   tablespoons chopped fresh garlic
6   fresh rosemary sprigs

1   fresh chive bunch

Mix goat cheese and sage in small bowl to blend. Season with salt and pepper. Cover and chill until ready to use.

Place lamb boned side up in baking pan. Rub garlic over lamb. Press rosemary sprigs into lamb. Let stand 1 hour at room temperature.

Preheat oven to 375°F. Bake lamb until thermometer registers 130°F for medium-rare, about 30 minutes. Cool 30 minutes. Cover lamb and chill overnight.

Remove rosemary from lamb. Cut lamb into paper-thin slices (if lamb is too soft to slice thinly, freeze briefly). Trim enough slices to make eighteen 3 x 2-inch rectangles.

Arrange lamb slices on work surface. Spread each slice with thin layer of cheese mixture. Starting at 1 short end, roll lamb up into cylinders. Tie centers with chives. Trim chive ends. Arrange bundles on platter. *(Can be prepared 4 hours ahead. Cover and keep refrigerated.)*

6 SERVINGS

◆ ◆ ◆

Any leftover lamb from this recipe can be used in sandwiches. Roasted almonds make a nice accompaniment to this sophisticated appetizer. Serve with an earthy, full-bodied Champagne or sparkling wine.

◆ ◆ ◆

Hot Artichoke and Tarragon Dip

◆ ◆ ◆

2   6-ounce jars marinated artichoke hearts, drained,
    coarsely chopped
½   cup mayonnaise
½   cup sour cream
½   cup grated Romano cheese
3   tablespoons chopped fresh tarragon or 1 tablespoon dried

Preheat oven to 350°F. Combine all ingredients in medium bowl. Transfer mixture to 3-cup ovenproof soufflé dish or small casserole. Bake dip until heated through, about 30 minutes.

MAKES 2 CUPS

Tomato, Cheese and Herb Tart

◆ ◆ ◆

1¼ cups all purpose flour
¼   teaspoon salt
½   cup (1 stick) chilled unsalted butter, cut into pieces
4   tablespoons (about) ice water

5   medium tomatoes, cut into ½-inch-thick slices

9   ounces Emmenthal or Gruyère cheese, thinly sliced
1   tablespoon minced fresh basil or 1 teaspoon dried
1   teaspoon minced fresh thyme or ¼ teaspoon dried
1   teaspoon minced fresh oregano or ¼ teaspoon dried
3   tablespoons freshly grated Parmesan cheese

FOR CRUST: Combine flour and salt in processor. Add butter and cut in using on/off turns until mixture resembles coarse meal. Add enough water by tablespoons to form moist clumps. Gather dough into ball; flatten into disk. Wrap in plastic and refrigerate 30 minutes.

Preheat oven to 375°F. Roll out dough on lightly floured surface

to 13-inch round. Transfer to 11-inch-diameter tart pan with removable bottom. Trim edges. Freeze crust 15 minutes.

Line crust with foil. Fill with dried beans or pie weights. Bake until crust is set, about 15 minutes. Remove foil and beans and bake until pale golden, about 15 minutes more. Cool crust on rack. *(Can be prepared 1 day ahead. Cover and let stand at room temperature.)*

FOR FILLING: Cut each tomato slice in half. Place tomato slices on paper towels and let drain 45 minutes.

Preheat oven to 375°F. Top crust with Emmenthal cheese slices. Arrange tomatoes atop cheese, overlapping slightly. Sprinkle herbs, then Parmesan cheese over tomatoes. Season with pepper. Bake until cheese melts and tomatoes are tender, about 35 minutes. Cool slightly. Remove tart pan sides. Cut tart into wedges and serve.

8 SERVINGS

Pita Bread with Hummus, Tomatoes and Mint

◆ ◆ ◆

1   15 ½-ounce can chick-peas (garbanzo beans), rinsed, drained
⅓   cup fresh lemon juice
⅓   cup tahini*
2   tablespoons water
½   teaspoon salt

1   large tomato, seeded, chopped
¼   cup chopped fresh mint
2   green onions, chopped

2   mini whole wheat pita breads

Combine first 5 ingredients in processor; puree. Season hummus with generous amount of pepper. *(Can be prepared 1 day ahead. Cover and refrigerate.)*

Combine tomato, mint and chopped green onions in bowl. Season with salt and pepper.

Toast pita breads until crisp. Spread each round generously with hummus. (Reserve remaining hummus for another use.) Top with tomato mixture. Cut each in half and serve.

*Tahini, sesame seed paste, is available at Middle Eastern and natural foods stores and some supermarkets.

2 SERVINGS

◆ ◆ ◆

This pita bread "tostada" is made with *hummus*, a middle Eastern chick-pea puree. It is a fine starter for a meatless menu, and is especially good with the Spicy Tofu and Vegetable Stir-fry with Soba Noodles on page 102.

◆ ◆ ◆

Fontina, Corn and Jalapeño Quesadillas

◆ ◆ ◆

2   *teaspoons olive oil*
1   *cup frozen corn kernels, thawed*
2   *jalapeño chilies, seeded, minced*
1   *teaspoon dried oregano, crumbled*

   Olive oil
8   *7-inch flour tortillas*
2   *cups grated Fontina cheese (about 8 ounces)*

Heat 2 teaspoons oil in heavy medium skillet over medium heat. Add corn, chilies and oregano and sauté 2 minutes. Remove from heat. *(Can be prepared 1 day ahead. Cover and refrigerate.)*

Heat clean heavy medium skillet over medium heat. Brush with oil. Add 1 tortilla. Cover with ½ cup cheese and ¼ of corn mixture. Top with another tortilla. Cook until tortillas are brown and cheese melts, about 2 minutes per side. Transfer to work surface. Repeat with remaining ingredients, forming 4 quesadillas in total. Cut each into 8 wedges.

4 SERVINGS

Mushroom Pirozhki

◆ ◆ ◆

1   *1-ounce package dried European or Polish mushrooms*

12 *ounces button mushrooms, quartered*
2   *tablespoons (¼ stick) butter*
1   *onion, chopped*
¾   *cup fresh breadcrumbs, preferably made from dark bread*
2   *tablespoons chopped fresh dill*

1   *15-ounce package All Ready Pie Crusts, room temperature*
1   *egg beaten with 1 teaspoon milk (glaze)*

Soak dried mushrooms in hot water 1 hour. Drain. Finely chop mushrooms.

Finely chop button mushrooms in processor. Melt butter in heavy large skillet over medium heat. Add onion; sauté until translucent, about 5 minutes. Add dried and fresh mushrooms and sauté

◆ ◆ ◆

These Russian turnovers are good with the Beef Borscht with Sour Cream and Dill on page 32.

◆ ◆ ◆

until mushrooms release their liquid, about 10 minutes. Add bread-crumbs and cook until mixture is thick and dry, stirring occasion-ally, about 5 minutes. Mix in dill. Season with salt and pepper. Cool.

Butter baking sheet. Roll out 1 pie crust on floured surface to 12- to 13-inch round. Using 3-inch-diameter cookie cutter, cut out rounds. Place 1 heaping teaspoon filling in center of each round. Brush edges with glaze. Bring 2 sides up to meet in center and pinch together, then press sealed edges against side of turnover, form-ing oval. Brush with glaze. Transfer to prepared sheet. Repeat with second crust, remaining filling and glaze. *(Can be made 1 day ahead. Cover and refrigerate.)*

Preheat oven to 350°F. Bake pirozhki until golden, about 30 minutes. Serve immediately.

MAKES ABOUT 2 DOZEN

Super-spiced Spiced Shrimp

◆ ◆ ◆

$\frac{1}{2}$ cup prepared horseradish
$\frac{1}{3}$ cup olive oil
$\frac{1}{4}$ cup Worcestershire sauce
$1\frac{1}{2}$ teaspoons hot pepper sauce (such as Tabasco)

2   quarts water
1   12-ounce bottle amber beer
10   small dried chilies (such as chili de arbol)
8   large garlic cloves, peeled
1   tablespoon yellow mustard seeds
4   bay leaves
2   pounds uncooked medium shrimp, peeled
1   large lemon, thinly sliced
1   tablespoon salt

Whisk first 4 ingredients to blend in bowl. *(Can be prepared 8 hours ahead. Cover and let stand at room temperature.)*

Bring water, beer, chilies, garlic, mustard seeds and bay leaves to boil in heavy large saucepan over high heat. Reduce heat to medium and simmer 10 minutes. Add shrimp, lemon and salt to beer mixture. Simmer until shrimp are just cooked through, about 3 min-utes. Pour shrimp mixture through large strainer, discarding liquids. Transfer contents of strainer to large bowl. Add horseradish mixture and stir to blend. Cool to room temperature, about 30 minutes.

8 SERVINGS

◆ ◆ ◆

Tingling lips, fingers worth licking and plenty of zesty flavor are the main rewards of this easy-to-eat starter. Serve with ice-cold beer, and don't forget the hot, damp towels to clean up with afterward.

◆ ◆ ◆

SPRINGTIME
DINNER FOR FOUR

FRESH WATERCRESS SOUP, PAGE 34

SWORDFISH WITH ONIONS,
RED PEPPERS AND LEMON-SAFFRON
SAUCE, PAGE 84

STEAMED GREEN BEANS

CHARDONNAY

CHILLED ESSENCIA SABAYON
WITH PINEAPPLE AND ORANGES,
PAGE 196

◆ ◆ ◆

Basic Chicken Stock

◆ ◆ ◆

4   pounds chicken wings
4   quarts cold water
3   celery stalks, sliced
1   large onion, sliced
1   large carrot, sliced
4   large fresh parsley sprigs
4   whole cloves
4   whole black peppercorns
1   teaspoon dried thyme, crumbled
1   bay leaf

Combine chicken wings and 4 quarts water in heavy large pot. Bring to boil over high heat. Reduce heat to medium-low and simmer 15 minutes, skimming foam from surface. Add remaining ingredients to pot; simmer 2 hours.

Strain stock, lightly pressing on solids to release all liquid. Chill stock until cold and fat on top is solid, at least 6 hours and up to 2 days. Discard fat on top.

Boil stock in heavy medium saucepan over high heat until reduced to 8 cups, about 30 minutes. *(Can be prepared ahead. Cover and refrigerate 2 days or freeze up to 6 months.)*

MAKES 8 CUPS

Corn Tortilla Chicken Soup.

Corn Tortilla Chicken Soup

♦ ♦ ♦

Vegetable oil for deep frying
8   *thin corn tortillas, halved, cut crosswise into thin strips*

1   *small onion, coarsely chopped*
2   *large garlic cloves, minced*
1   *tablespoon chili powder*
2   *teaspoons ground cumin*
1/2 *teaspoon dried oregano, crumbled*
1   *bay leaf*
6   *cups Basic Chicken Stock (see recipe, page 26) or canned*
     low-salt broth
1   *8-ounce can tomato sauce*
1 1/2 *teaspoons salt*
1   *teaspoon sugar*
1/4 *teaspoon ground pepper*
2   *large chicken breast halves (about 1 1/2 pounds)*

1 1/2 *cups fresh corn kernels (from about 2 ears) or frozen,*
     thawed

Sour cream
Sliced radishes
Chopped fresh cilantro
Finely chopped red onion

Pour oil into heavy medium skillet to depth of ¾ inch and heat oil to 350°F. Fry tortilla strips in batches until crisp and golden, about 1 minute. Drain tortillas on paper towels.

Transfer 1 tablespoon tortilla-frying oil to heavy large pot. Add onion and sauté over medium heat until tender, about 5 minutes. Add garlic, chili powder, cumin, oregano and bay leaf. Sauté 1 minute. Add chicken stock, tomato sauce, salt, sugar and pepper and bring to boil. Add chicken. Cover pot and simmer until chicken is just cooked through, about 15 minutes.

Using tongs, transfer chicken to plate and cool slightly. Cut away skin and bones from chicken; shred finely. Add 1¼ cups of corn to soup. Simmer until corn is tender, about 5 minutes. Add chicken to soup and simmer 1 minute. *(Can be prepared 1 day ahead. Cover and refrigerate. Bring just to simmer before continuing.)*

Ladle soup into bowls. Garnish with tortilla strips, sour cream, radishes, cilantro, red onion and remaining ¼ cup corn kernels.

6 SERVINGS

♦ ♦ ♦

This Mexican-inspired soup is colorful, festive and fragrant. It's also a great do-ahead recipe.

♦ ♦ ♦

Chinese Hot-and-Sour Soup

◆ ◆ ◆

This classic Szechuan soup is usually prepared with pork; here, chicken breast makes a deliciously light and lean version. Serve with hot, crusty bread and a salad of Napa cabbage and red cabbage with a rice-vinegar-based dressing.

◆ ◆ ◆

1   ounce dried shiitake mushrooms
1   cup boiling water

½   pound fresh snow peas, trimmed, cut diagonally into thin strips

6   cups Basic Chicken Stock (see recipe, page 26) or canned low-salt broth
2   tablespoons minced peeled fresh ginger
1   large garlic clove, minced
1½ cups diced well-drained firm tofu (about 10 ounces)
1   8-ounce can sliced bamboo shoots, drained, cut into strips
1   medium-size red bell pepper, thinly sliced
4   ounces button mushrooms, thinly sliced (about 1½ cups)

¼   cup dry Sherry
3   tablespoons rice vinegar
3   tablespoons soy sauce
½   teaspoon dried crushed red pepper
2   teaspoons sugar
¼   cup cold water
3   tablespoons cornstarch
2   skinless boneless chicken breast halves, cut crosswise into ¼-inch-wide strips
2   teaspoons oriental sesame oil
6   green onions, thinly sliced

Place dried mushrooms in medium bowl. Pour 1 cup boiling water over. Let stand until mushrooms soften, about 30 minutes. Drain, reserving soaking liquid. Trim stems; thinly slice mushrooms.

Blanch snow peas in medium pot of boiling salted water 1 minute. Drain thoroughly.

Bring chicken stock, reserved mushroom-soaking liquid, ginger and garlic to boil in large pot. Reduce heat to low, cover and simmer 10 minutes. Add tofu, bamboo shoots, red bell pepper, sliced button mushrooms and shiitake mushrooms. Simmer soup uncovered for 8 minutes.

Mix Sherry, vinegar, soy sauce, crushed red pepper and sugar into soup. Season generously with black pepper. Return soup to simmer. Mix ¼ cup cold water and cornstarch in small bowl until smooth. Add cornstarch mixture and chicken to soup and simmer until thickened, about 2 minutes. Remove from heat. Mix in sesame oil. Season with salt. *(Can be prepared 1 day ahead. Cover soup and snow peas separately and refrigerate. Bring to simmer.)* Ladle soup into bowls. Garnish with snow peas and onions.

8 SERVINGS

Carrot and Caraway Soup

◆ ◆ ◆

1   tablespoon butter
1   onion, chopped
12   ounces carrots, peeled, sliced
1   teaspoon caraway seeds, crushed in mortar with pestle
1   14½-ounce can (or more) chicken broth

2   tablespoons aquavit (caraway spirit)
     Chopped fresh parsley

Melt butter in heavy medium saucepan over medium heat. Add onion and sauté 1 minute. Add carrots and sauté until onion is tender, about 8 minutes. Add caraway and cook 30 seconds. Add 1 can broth. Cover and simmer until carrots are tender, about 35 minutes.

Puree soup in processor. Season to taste with salt and pepper. *(Can be prepared 1 day ahead. Cover and refrigerate.)* Return soup to saucepan and bring to simmer, thinning with more broth if too thick. Mix in aquavit. Ladle into bowls. Garnish with chopped parsley and serve immediately.

2 SERVINGS

◆ ◆ ◆

A splash of the caraway–flavored Danish spirit aquavit is the finishing touch to this practically-no-fat starter.

◆ ◆ ◆

No-Cream Asparagus Soup

◆ ◆ ◆

2   tablespoons (¼ stick) butter
2   medium onions, chopped
2   medium leeks (white and pale green parts only), chopped
6   cups chicken stock or canned low-salt broth
2   pounds asparagus, ends trimmed, each cut into 4 pieces

Melt butter in large pot over medium heat. Add onions and leeks; sauté until tender, about 15 minutes. Add stock and asparagus; simmer until asparagus are tender, about 15 minutes. Puree soup in blender in batches. Return to pot. Season with salt and pepper. *(Can be made 1 day ahead. Cover; chill.)* Bring to simmer before serving, stirring occasionally.

MAKES ABOUT 8 CUPS

Potato, Lentil and Wild Mushroom Soup

◆ ◆ ◆

1   ounce dried porcini mushrooms
1   cup boiling water

2   tablespoons olive oil
1½   cups chopped shallots
2   pounds russet potatoes, peeled, cut into ½- to ¾-inch pieces
4   14½-ounce cans beef broth
¾   pound fully cooked reduced-fat sausage (such as kielbasa), cut in half lengthwise
1¼   cups lentils, rinsed, drained
1¼   teaspoons dried thyme, crumbled

Place porcini mushrooms in bowl; add water. Let mushrooms stand until soft, about 20 minutes.

Heat oil in large pot over medium heat. Add shallots; sauté until soft, about 5 minutes. Add potatoes, broth, sausage, lentils and thyme. Add mushrooms to soup, reserving liquid.

Strain mushroom soaking liquid to remove any sediment; add liquid to soup. Cook soup until potatoes and lentils are tender and soup is thick, stirring occasionally, about 1 hour 15 minutes.

Transfer sausage to plate and slice. Transfer 1½ cups soup to blender and puree. Return puree and sausage to soup. Season with salt and pepper. *(Can be prepared 2 days ahead. Cover and refrigerate. Reheat before serving.)*

6 TO 8 SERVINGS

Fennel, Apple and Almond Soup

◆ ◆ ◆

2 tablespoons walnut or olive oil
1 8-ounce fennel bulb, sliced
1 small onion, chopped
1 8-ounce tart green apple, peeled, cored, chopped
1 6-ounce celery root, peeled, chopped
2½ cups chicken broth
½ cup whipping cream
2 tablespoons ground toasted almonds
   Pinch of ground nutmeg

2 tablespoons toasted sliced almonds
   Fennel fronds

Heat oil in Dutch oven over medium heat. Add fennel and onion and sauté until softened, about 5 minutes. Mix in apple, celery root and broth. Bring to simmer. Cover and cook until vegetables are soft, about 30 minutes. Working in batches, transfer mixture to blender. Puree until smooth. Add whipping cream, ground almonds and nutmeg. Season to taste with salt and pepper. *(Can be prepared 1 day ahead. Cover tightly and refrigerate.)*

Reheat soup. Ladle into bowls. Top each serving with sliced almonds and fennel fronds.

MAKES ABOUT 5½ CUPS

Beef Borscht with
Sour Cream and Dill

◆ ◆ ◆

2   tablespoons (¹/₄ stick) butter
4³/₄ pounds beef chuck pot roast, cut into 2-inch chunks, fat
     trimmed, bones reserved
6   cups chopped green cabbage
3   celery stalks, chopped
2   large onions, chopped
2   large carrots, chopped
4   14¹/₂-ounce cans beef broth
2   14¹/₂-ounce cans diced peeled tomatoes, with juices

4   large red-skinned potatoes, peeled, cut into ¹/₂-inch pieces

2   16-ounce cans julienne beets, with juices
2¹/₂ tablespoons cider vinegar
1   tablespoon sugar
     Sour cream
     Chopped fresh dill

Melt butter in heavy 8-quart pot over high heat. Working in
batches, add beef and bones and brown on all sides. Transfer to
plate. Add cabbage, celery, onions and carrots to pot and sauté until

Beef Borscht with Sour Cream and Dill
and Mushroom Pirozhki, page 22.

tender, about 15 minutes. Return meat, bones and any juices to pot. Add broth and tomatoes. Bring to boil. Reduce heat, cover and simmer soup for 1 hour.

Add potatoes to soup, cover and simmer until tender, about 30 minutes. Discard bones. Remove meat and cut into small bite-size pieces; return to soup. Cover and refrigerate overnight.

Skim fat from surface of soup. Bring soup to boil. Add beets; heat through. Add vinegar and sugar. Season with salt and pepper. Ladle into bowls. Top with dollop of sour cream; sprinkle with dill.

8 SERVINGS

Curried Squash Soup

◆ ◆ ◆

4   pounds butternut squash (about 2 large), halved, seeded

$^1/_4$ cup ($^1/_2$ stick) unsalted butter

2   cups chopped onion

5   teaspoons curry powder

$^1/_4$ teaspoon ground allspice

4   cups chicken stock or canned low-salt broth

1   cup half and half

$^1/_4$ cup chopped chives

Preheat oven to 350°F. Place squash cut side down on baking sheet. Bake until soft, about 50 minutes. Scoop out squash pulp; discard squash skin.

Melt butter in heavy large skillet over medium heat. Add onion, curry and allspice and sauté until onion is tender, about 10 minutes. Transfer $^1/_4$ of onion mixture, $^1/_4$ of squash and 1 cup stock to blender; puree. Pour into heavy large saucepan. Puree remaining onion mixture, squash and stock in blender in 3 more batches. Add to saucepan. Add half and half to soup; bring to boil, stirring occasionally. Reduce heat and simmer 10 minutes. Season to taste with salt and pepper. *(Can be made 1 day ahead. Cover and refrigerate. Bring to simmer before serving.)* Mix chives into soup.

12 SERVINGS

Some noted party givers share their tips for mixing good times with good sense.

"When entertaining, I always abide by what I learned in hotel school in Switzerland: Nothing is more vulgar than too much food on a plate." *Craig Claiborne, food critic and cookbook author*

"Healthful entertaining starts in the marketplace. Go for what's in season, because the flavors will pop out at you when ingredients are at their ripest." *Allen Susser, chef-owner of Chef Allen's in North Miami Beach*

"Entertaining healthfully is more about what you don't do to food. The less you fuss, the more you get healthful dishes that taste fresh and look appealing." *Jill St. John, actress and cookbook author*

"One way to healthfully enliven the cocktail hour is to serve drinks made with fresh fruit or vegetables instead of alcohol. Like most natural foods, fruits and vegetables can be blended almost any way and taste terrific." *Julee Rosso, cookbook author and innkeeper*

◆ ◆ ◆

Cold Avocado and Tomato Soup

◆ ◆ ◆

2   ripe avocados, halved, peeled
³/₄ cup buttermilk
1   10-ounce cucumber, peeled, halved, seeded, cut into pieces
2   large green onions (including green tops), chopped
¹/₄ cup (or more) canned chicken broth

1   pound ripe tomatoes, halved, seeded, quartered
1   cup packed roasted red bell peppers (from jar)
1   tablespoon sugar
1   tablespoon fresh tarragon leaves

   Sour cream
   Fresh tarragon sprigs

Place first 4 ingredients in processor. Blend until smooth. Add ¹/₄ cup broth. Season to taste with salt and pepper. Blend to mix. Transfer soup to bowl. Cover and refrigerate.

Place tomatoes, bell peppers and sugar in clean processor. Blend until smooth. Add tarragon leaves. Season with salt and pepper. Blend 30 seconds. Transfer to bowl. Cover and chill. *(Both soups can be made 4 hours ahead.)*

If avocado soup is very thick, thin slightly with more broth. Ladle both soups simultaneously into each soup bowl. Garnish each with dollop of sour cream and tarragon sprig.

MAKES ABOUT 5 CUPS

Fresh Watercress Soup

◆ ◆ ◆

2   tablespoons (¹/₄ stick) unsalted butter
1   large onion, chopped
3   large garlic cloves, chopped
4   cups chicken stock or canned low-salt broth
1   large russet potato (about 9 ounces), peeled, cut into ¹/₂-inch pieces
4   cups packed trimmed watercress (about 4 large bunches)
¹/₃ cup whipping cream

   Additional whipping cream
4   watercress leaves

Melt butter in heavy large saucepan over medium-low heat. Add onion and garlic and sauté until tender, about 10 minutes. Mix in stock and potato. Cover and simmer until potato is very tender, about 15 minutes. Add 4 cups watercress and simmer just until wilted and tender, about 4 minutes. Remove from heat. Stir in $1/3$ cup cream. Puree soup in blender in batches until smooth. Return puree to saucepan. Season to taste with salt and pepper. *(Can be prepared 1 day ahead. Cover and refrigerate.)*

Bring soup to simmer. Ladle into bowls. Drizzle with cream and garnish with watercress leaves.

4 SERVINGS

Chilled Red Pepper Soup with Basil and Croutons

◆ ◆ ◆

4   large red bell peppers (about $2^{1}/_{4}$ pounds total)

4   tablespoons olive oil
1   onion, cut into $3/_{4}$-inch pieces
3   cups (or more) chicken stock or canned broth
$1/_{8}$ teaspoon dried crushed red pepper

$1^{1}/_{2}$ cups $1/_{2}$-inch French bread cubes
     Fresh basil leaves, slivered

Char peppers over gas flame or in broiler until blackened on all sides. Wrap in paper bag and let stand 10 minutes. Peel and seed. Cut into $1/_{2}$-inch pieces.

Heat 2 tablespoons oil in heavy large saucepan over medium-high heat. Add onion and sauté until brown on edges, about 6 minutes. Add bell peppers and 3 cups stock. Simmer until vegetables are tender, about 5 minutes. Using slotted spoon, transfer peppers and onion to processor; puree. With machine running, add stock from saucepan and blend until smooth. Mix in dried red pepper. Season with salt and pepper. Cover soup and refrigerate until cold. *(Can be prepared 1 day ahead.)*

Heat 2 tablespoons oil in medium skillet over medium heat. Add bread; stir until brown. Whisk cold soup to blend; thin with more stock if necessary. Spoon into bowls. Top with bread and basil.

4 SERVINGS

◆ ◆ ◆

HOT DRINKS FOR COLD-WEATHER PARTIES

◆ ◆ ◆

*Clockwise from near right: Swedish
Mulled Wine; Triple Apple Mulled
Cider; Tea Soother; Groddy; Raichlen's
Remedy; Cranberry Rose Punch.*

◆ BEVERAGES ◆

The Sunrise

◆ ◆ ◆

1   *cup fresh orange juice*
$^{1}/_{4}$ *cup fresh lime juice*
1   *tablespoon honey*
    Pinch of nutmeg

Mix all ingredients thoroughly in blender.

MAKES ABOUT 1 $^{1}/_{3}$ CUPS

Blackberry Lemonade

◆ ◆ ◆

3   *$^{1}/_{2}$-pint baskets fresh blackberries or one 16-ounce package*
    frozen unsweetened blackberries, thawed
12   *cups water*
2   *12-ounce containers frozen lemonade concentrate, thawed*
3   *tablespoons (or more) sugar*

    Ice cubes
    Lemon slices
    Fresh mint sprigs

Puree berries in processor. Strain through sieve, pressing on solids with back of spoon. Transfer to large pitcher. Add 12 cups water, lemonade concentrate and 3 tablespoons sugar. Taste, adding more sugar if desired. Cover and chill until very cold. *(Lemonade can be prepared up to 1 day ahead.)*

Fill glasses with ice. Pour lemonade over. Garnish with lemon slices and mint sprigs.

12 SERVINGS

Springtime Mimosas

♦ ♦ ♦

$1^{1}/_{2}$ cups fresh blood orange juice or regular orange juice
6 teaspoons crème de cassis
1 750-ml bottle chilled sparkling wine
6 orange peel strips

Pour $^{1}/_{4}$ cup juice into each of 6 glasses. Add 1 teaspoon crème de cassis to each. Fill with sparkling wine. Garnish with peel.

MAKES 6

Cranberry Rose Punch

♦ ♦ ♦

$2^{1}/_{4}$ cups water
4 cinnamon tea bags
2 cinnamon sticks
2 cups cranberry juice cocktail
3 tablespoons (or more) honey
1 tablespoon fresh lime juice
$^{1}/_{2}$ teaspoon rose water* (optional)

Bring water to boil in heavy medium saucepan. Add tea bags and cinnamon. Remove from heat. Cover and let steep 10 minutes. Remove tea bags. Add cranberry juice to tea mixture and bring to simmer. Mix in 3 tablespoons honey, lime juice and rose water, if desired. Taste; add more honey, if desired.

*Rose water is available at liquor stores, specialty foods stores and some supermarkets.

4 SERVINGS

WASHINGTON APPLES

Many of us eat an apple a day without ever stopping to think about where it came from or how it got to the market. If you had one today, chances are it came from Washington. Last year the average American ate more than 13 pounds' worth of fresh apples from the Evergreen State, and that adds up to more than half of the total national consumption. In the foothills of the Yakima Valley, east of the Cascade Mountains, farmers tend nearly 31 million apple trees on about 180,000 acres of orchard.

While Red Delicious is the undisputed champion among Washington's varieties, accounting for two of every three apples harvested, the state also grows Granny Smith, Golden Delicious, Rome Beauty, Winesap, Jonathan and Newton Pippin apples.

◆ ◆ ◆

Groddy

◆ ◆ ◆

8   *tablespoons Irish whiskey*
8   *tablespoons Irish Mist or other whiskey liqueur*
6   *tablespoons fresh lemon juice*
4   *tablespoons honey*
2   *cups boiling water*
4   *cinnamon sticks*

Measure 2 tablespoons whiskey, 2 tablespoons Irish Mist, 1½ tablespoons lemon juice and 1 tablespoon honey into each of 4 mugs. Pour ½ cup boiling water into each mug. Place 1 cinnamon stick in each mug and serve.

4 SERVINGS

Triple Apple Mulled Cider

◆ ◆ ◆

½   *orange*
½   *lemon*
2   *cinnamon sticks*
5   *whole cloves*
3   *whole allspice berries*
4   *cups apple cider*
2   *cups hard cider* (such as Taunton or Woodpecker) or apple cider*
1   *cup ginger ale*
1   *cup dried apples, diced*
½   *cup (or more) firmly packed brown sugar*
⅛   *teaspoon ground mace*

1   *cup Calvados or applejack*
8   *crystallized ginger slices*

Using vegetable peeler, remove peel (colored part only) in strips from orange and lemon halves. Place peel, cinnamon, cloves and allspice berries on cheesecloth square and tie to close. Place in large saucepan. Add both ciders, ginger ale, apples, ½ cup brown sugar and ground mace. Squeeze juice from orange and lemon into cider mixture. Bring almost to simmer, stirring occasionally. Reduce heat to low; cook 20 minutes, skimming off foam that rises to surface. Remove cheese cloth bundle. Taste cider; add more brown sugar, if desired.

Pour 2 tablespoons Calvados into each mug. Ladle cider into mugs. Attach 1 ginger slice to rim of each mug.

* Available at some liquor stores and some specialty foods stores.

8 SERVINGS

Swedish Mulled Wine

◆ ◆ ◆

1   *orange*

1   *lemon*

1$^1/_2$ *cinnamon sticks*

6   *whole cardamom pods*

3   *whole cloves*

1   *1$^1/_2$-inch-long fresh ginger piece, thinly sliced*

1   *750-ml bottle dry red wine*

1   *375-ml bottle late harvest Riesling or other sweet dessert wine*

$^1/_2$ *cup golden raisins*

$^1/_2$ *cup dried sour cherries,* dried cranberries or currants*

$^1/_2$ *cup blanched slivered almonds*

$^1/_4$ *cup (or more) sugar*

1$^1/_2$ *teaspoons Angostura bitters*

$^1/_2$ *cup aquavit (caraway spirit)*

Using vegetable peeler, remove peel (colored part only) in strips from orange and lemon. Place strips on cheesecloth square. Add cinnamon, cardamom, cloves and ginger and tie to close. Place in heavy large saucepan. Add both wines, raisins, sour cherries, almonds, $^1/_4$ cup sugar and bitters and bring almost to a simmer. Reduce heat to low and cook 20 minutes. Remove cheesecloth bundle. Taste mulled wine and add more sugar, if desired.

Just before servings, transfer hot mulled wine to heatproof bowl. Spoon aquavit over; ignite with match. When flames subside, ladle wine, fruits and nuts into mugs. Serve with spoons.

*Available at specialty foods stores and some supermarkets.

6 SERVINGS

◆ ◆ ◆

Centuries ago, medieval monarchs quaffed hippocras, red wine flavored with "mulled" (freshly milled or ground) spices like cloves, nutmeg and allspice berries. Believed to possess medicinal virtues, the drink was named for the Greek physician Hippocrates. Today this concoction survives as *glogg*, a hot mulled wine fortified with spices, nuts and dried fruits, popular in Sweden. The recipe at left is a delicious example.

◆ ◆ ◆

This drink is named after its creator, Steven Raichlen, a cookbook author, columnist and cooking teacher, as well as a contributor to *Bon Appétit*. Steven's remedy is guaranteed to cure the blahs. You can use any eau-de-vie, such as framboise (clear raspberry brandy), kirsch (clear cherry brandy), or poire Williams (clear pear brandy).

◆ ◆ ◆

Raichlen's Remedy

◆ ◆ ◆

6   tablespoons eau-de-vie
2   tablespoons fresh lemon juice
2   tablespoons sugar
1   cup boiling water
    Fresh raspberries or frozen, thawed (optional)

Divide eau-de-vie, lemon juice and sugar between 2 mugs. Add boiling water and stir to dissolve sugar. Garnish drinks with berries, if desired. Serve immediately.

2 SERVINGS

Tea Soother

◆ ◆ ◆

1   lemon
4 ½   cups water
16   whole cardamom pods
12   whole black peppercorns
8   whole cloves
4   heaping teaspoons Earl Grey tea or 4 tea bags
¼   cup sweetened condensed milk
      Sugar
      Lemon slices

Using vegetable peeler, remove peel (yellow part only) in strips from lemon. Place in heavy medium saucepan. Add 4 ½ cups water, cardamom, peppercorns and cloves and bring to simmer. Reduce heat to very low. Cover and let barely simmer 15 minutes. Increase heat and bring mixture to boil. Add tea. Remove from heat. Cover and let steep 5 minutes. Mix in sweetened condensed milk. Sweeten to taste with sugar. Strain into cups. Garnish with lemon slices.

6 SERVINGS

Ginger-spiced Tea

◆ ◆ ◆

6   *cups water*
6   *whole cardamom pods*
4   *fresh or crystallized ginger slices*
2   *1½ x 3-inch orange peel strips (orange part only)*
6   *whole cloves*
2   *cups low-fat milk*
6   *teaspoons tea leaves (preferably Darjeeling or Assam)*
¼   *cup packed dark brown sugar*

Combine first 5 ingredients in heavy large saucepan. Cover and simmer 10 minutes. Add milk and tea, bring to boil and simmer 2 minutes. Turn off heat and steep 4 to 6 minutes, according to desired strength. Mix in sugar. Strain tea. *(Can be prepared 6 hours ahead. Cover and chill. Rewarm before serving.)*

6 SERVINGS

Spirited Coffee

◆ ◆ ◆

½ cup milk
1 cup hot espresso or strong coffee
2 tablespoons coffee liqueur
½ teaspoon sambuca or other licorice-flavored liqueur
1½ teaspoons brandy

Scald milk in heavy small saucepan. Whisk hot milk until slightly thickened and frothy. Combine espresso, liqueurs and brandy. Divide between mugs or cups. Spoon frothy milk atop espresso.

2 SERVINGS

◆ Main Courses ◆

The main course is the centerpiece of most every meal. It's the dish we decide on first when planning a menu, setting the tone and mood for the rest of the meal. It's "What's cooking?," "What's for dinner?," and "What's to eat?," and it's what this chapter is all about.

The recipes here are divided into five sections — meats, poultry, seafood, meatless and pasta and pizza — to make finding the ideal dish easy. Of course if you don't have anything specific in mind, the chapter lends itself to browsing, too. Window-shop your way through what we think is a great collection of entrées that work for every occasion, from a simple after-work supper (say, Spinach-stuffed Chicken Breasts, page 70) to a sophisticated Saturday night dinner party (maybe Crown Roast of Lamb with Shallots, Mustard and Mint, page 55). There's a centerpiece for every table and every taste.

Tarragon-Butter Roast Chicken with Mushroom Sauce, page 64; Tarragon-Butter Sautéed Potatoes, page 132.

Wine-braised Beef
over Creamy Polenta

◆ ◆ ◆

3   tablespoons olive oil (preferably extra-virgin)
7   pounds beef chuck roast, trimmed, boned, cut into 1-inch
      cubes
1   large onion, minced
¼   cup chopped fresh Italian parsley
3   garlic cloves, chopped
2   bay leaves
¼   teaspoon ground cloves
¼   teaspoon ground cinnamon
¼   teaspoon ground allspice

1   cup dry red wine
2¼ cups beef stock or canned broth
2   14- to 16-ounce cans whole Italian plum tomatoes
½   cup pitted Niçoise olives*
4   teaspoons chopped fresh rosemary or 2 teaspoons dried
2   red bell peppers, cut into ¼-inch-wide strips

9   cups water
1½ teaspoons salt
2   cups cornmeal

FOR BEEF: Heat oil in heavy Dutch oven over high heat. Add ⅕ of beef and brown on all sides, stirring occasionally, about 5 minutes. Transfer beef to bowl using slotted spoon. Repeat with remaining beef in 4 more batches. Reduce heat to medium. Add onion and Italian parsley to Dutch oven and cook until onion is golden brown, stirring frequently, about 10 minutes. Stir in chopped garlic, bay leaves, cloves, cinnamon and allspice.

Return beef to Dutch oven and stir to coat with onion and spice mixture. Add red wine and bring to boil, scraping up any browned bits. Simmer mixture 15 minutes. Add beef stock and simmer 10 minutes. Add tomatoes with their juices, breaking up tomatoes with back

of spoon. Mix in olives and rosemary. Reduce heat to low, cover and cook until beef is tender, stirring occasionally, about 1½ hours. Add bell peppers, cover and cook until just tender, about 15 minutes. Season to taste with salt and pepper. *(Can be prepared 1 day ahead. Cover and refrigerate.)*

FOR POLENTA: Bring water and salt to boil in heavy large saucepan. Gradually whisk in cornmeal. Continue whisking until mixture boils and thickens, about 2 minutes. Reduce heat to low. Cook cornmeal until thick and thoroughly cooked, whisking occasionally, about 30 minutes. *(Polenta can be prepared up to 4 hours ahead. Transfer to metal bowl. Cover tightly with aluminum foil. Set bowl over large saucepan of barely simmering water. Stir occasionally.)*

Bring beef to simmer, stirring occasionally. Spoon polenta into shallow soup bowls. Spoon beef over.

*Small, brine-cured black olives, available at specialty foods stores and in some supermarkets.

6 SERVINGS

Top Sirloin Steak with Bell Pepper and Onion Sauté

◆ ◆ ◆

2   1½-pound top sirloin steaks (or one 2- to 3-pound steak),
    1 inch thick
6   tablespoons olive oil
2   tablespoons balsamic vinegar or red wine vinegar
6   garlic cloves, minced

1   large onion, sliced
1   large red bell pepper, sliced
1   large green bell pepper, sliced
1   cup unsalted beef broth or low-salt chicken broth

    Crumbled Gorgonzola or other blue cheese
    Minced fresh Italian parsley

Place steaks in glass baking dish. Mix 4 tablespoons oil, vinegar and half of garlic in small bowl. Pour over steaks; turn to coat. Marinate 30 minutes at room temperature or refrigerate 3 hours.

Heat 2 tablespoons oil in heavy large skillet over medium heat. Add onion, bell peppers and remaining garlic and sauté 8 minutes. Add broth, increase heat and boil until vegetables are tender and liquid thickens slightly, about 5 minutes. Season with salt and pepper. *(Can be prepared 3 hours ahead. Cover and chill.)*

Prepare barbecue (high heat) or preheat broiler. Remove steaks from marinade. Sprinkle with salt and generous amount of pepper. Grill steaks until cooked as desired, about 5 minutes per side for rare. Transfer steaks to platter and let stand 5 minutes. Bring vegetables to simmer. Slice steaks; arrange on platter. Top with vegetables and skillet juices. Sprinkle with cheese and parsley.

4 SERVINGS

Top Sirloin Steak with Bell Pepper and Onion Sauté; Double-Tomato Salad, page 147; Chili Potatoes, page 129.

Beef Stew with Mushrooms and Red Wine

◆ ◆ ◆

<table>
<tr><td>3</td><td>tablespoons (or more) vegetable oil</td></tr>
<tr><td></td><td>All purpose flour</td></tr>
<tr><td>2 1/2</td><td>pounds boneless beef chuck, cut into 1 1/2-inch cubes</td></tr>
<tr><td>1</td><td>garlic clove, minced</td></tr>
<tr><td>2</td><td>cups dry red wine</td></tr>
<tr><td>3/4</td><td>cup (about) beef stock or canned broth</td></tr>
<tr><td>3</td><td>fresh parsley sprigs</td></tr>
<tr><td>1</td><td>bay leaf</td></tr>
<tr><td>2</td><td>bacon slices, chopped</td></tr>
<tr><td>1</td><td>cup coarsely chopped onion</td></tr>
<tr><td>1</td><td>tablespoon tomato paste</td></tr>
<tr><td>2</td><td>tablespoons (1/4 stick) butter</td></tr>
<tr><td>1</td><td>pound mushrooms, quartered</td></tr>
<tr><td></td><td>Fresh chopped parsley</td></tr>
</table>

Preheat oven to 325°F. Heat 3 tablespoons oil in heavy large Dutch oven over high heat. Place flour in medium bowl; season with salt and pepper. Coat beef with flour, shaking off excess. Add half of beef to Dutch oven and brown well on all sides, about 5 minutes. Transfer beef to plate. Repeat with remaining beef, adding more oil to pan as necessary. Return beef and any accumulated juices to Dutch oven. Reduce heat to medium. Add garlic and cook 1 minute. Add wine and enough beef stock to cover meat. Add parsley sprigs and bay leaf. Cover and bake about 2 hours.

Heat heavy small skillet over high heat. Add bacon and sauté until crisp. Transfer bacon to paper towels, using slotted spoon. Add onion to skillet and sauté until translucent, about 5 minutes. Add tomato paste; stir 2 minutes. Add bacon and onion mixture to stew. Thin liquid with more stock if necessary. Cover and bake until meat is tender, about 30 minutes.

Melt butter in heavy large skillet over high heat. Add mushrooms and sauté until tender, about 10 minutes. Add mushrooms to stew. Season with salt and pepper. *(Can be made 1 day ahead. Cover and chill. Rewarm in 325°F oven about 30 minutes.)* Ladle stew into bowls. Sprinkle with chopped parsley.

+ TO 6 SERVINGS

STRATEGY FOR A GETAWAY DINNER

If you're going away for the weekend — to a cabin, condo or second home — and want to make supper on Saturday night, here are a few tips to help you plan ahead.

◆ Keep the menu simple and appropriate to the surroundings. A fancy, candlelit dinner, for instance, would seem out of place at a cabin in the mountains.

◆ Don't plan on preparing anything that requires the kind of special cooking equipment you might need to bring from home.

◆ Plan the menu, make a shopping list, then buy all the ingredients on Friday. If your weekend destination involves more than half an hour's driving time, pack all perishables in an ice chest.

◆ Remember to bring along beverages, paper goods and utensils, if necessary.

◆ ◆ ◆

Braised Short Ribs with Root Vegetables

◆ ◆ ◆

5   tablespoons (about) olive oil

1¹/₂ large onions, chopped

4   garlic cloves, minced
     All purpose flour (for coating)

4   pounds beef short ribs

1¹/₂ cups dry red wine

¹/₄ cup tomato paste

3   cups canned beef broth

2   bay leaves

5   tablespoons chopped fresh marjoram or 1¹/₂ tablespoons
     dried

2   turnips, peeled, cut into 1¹/₂-inch pieces

2   large russet potatoes, peeled, cut into 1¹/₂-inch pieces

4   large carrots, peeled, cut into 2-inch pieces

Heat 2 tablespoons oil in heavy Dutch oven over medium-high heat. Add onions and garlic and sauté until tender, about 10 minutes. Using slotted spoon, transfer to plate. Season flour with salt and pepper. Turn short ribs in flour to coat; shake off excess. Add 3 tablespoons oil to Dutch oven and heat over high heat. Add short ribs and cook until brown on all sides, about 10 minutes. Transfer short ribs to plate. Pour off fat from Dutch oven.

Return onion mixture to Dutch oven. Add wine and boil until very thick, scraping up any browned bits, about 8 minutes. Stir in tomato paste, then broth, bay leaves and half of marjoram. Return ribs to Dutch oven and bring to boil. Reduce heat, cover and simmer 1 hour 30 minutes.

Add turnips, potatoes and carrots to short ribs. Cover and simmer until vegetables and meat are tender, about 50 minutes longer. Uncover and simmer until sauce thickens, stirring frequently, about 10 minutes. Season with salt and pepper. *(Can be prepared 1 day ahead. Cover and refrigerate. Rewarm.)* Sprinkle with remaining marjoram and then serve.

4 SERVINGS

◆ ◆ ◆

A robust one-dish meal. Offer sourdough bread alongside and serve with a Zinfandel or Pinot Noir.

Braised Short Ribs with Root Vegetables and Romaine Salad.

Veal Chops with Mustard Sage Sauce

◆ ◆ ◆

1½ tablespoons butter

1   teaspoon vegetable oil

2   1-inch-thick veal loin chops
     Dried rubbed sage

2½ tablespoons chopped shallots

⅓   cup unsalted beef broth

2   tablespoons minced fresh sage or 2 teaspoons dried rubbed

2   teaspoons Dijon mustard

¼   cup half and half
     Fresh sage leaves

Melt butter with oil in heavy medium skillet over medium-high heat. Sprinkle chops with dried sage and pepper. Add to skillet and cook until brown, about 5 minutes per side. Reduce heat to medium and cook to desired doneness, about 1 minute per side for medium-rare. Transfer veal to plate; keep warm.

Add shallots to same skillet and stir 1 minute. Add broth, 1 tablespoon minced sage and mustard to skillet and boil until very thick, scraping up browned bits, about 4 minutes. Add half and half and boil until liquid thickens to sauce consistency, about 1 minute. Mix in remaining 1 tablespoon minced sage and any juices exuded by veal. Adjust seasoning. Place 1 chop on each plate. Spoon sauce over. Garnish with fresh sage leaves and serve.

2 SERVINGS

Veal Chops with Mustard Sage Sauce; Roasted Potatoes and Steamed Green Beans; Carrot and Caraway Soup, page 29; Berry Napoleons, page 173.

Roast Veal Brisket with Marsala-Mushroom Sauce

◆ ◆ ◆

2   6- to 7-pound point-end veal breasts, boned, fat trimmed (about 2 1/2 pounds each after boning), bones reserved and cut into pieces
     Dried thyme
1 1/2 pounds medium onions, quartered
2   tablespoons all purpose flour

1 1/2 pounds button mushrooms, thickly sliced
4   cups chicken stock or canned low-salt broth
2   cups dry imported Marsala
2   ounces dried porcini mushrooms, rinsed, drained
8   large garlic cloves
1/4 teaspoon (generous) ground allspice

     Fresh thyme (optional)

Preheat oven to 350°F. Season veal generously with dried thyme, salt and pepper. Heat heavy large skillet over high heat. Add veal bones and cook until some fat is rendered, turning occasionally, about 5 minutes. Add onions and sauté until brown, about 15 minutes. Sprinkle flour over and stir 3 minutes. Transfer mixture to large roasting pan, spreading onions in center and bones around edge. Add 1 brisket to same skillet and cook until brown, about 5 minutes per side. Place atop onions. Repeat with second brisket.

Add button mushrooms, stock, Marsala, dried mushrooms, garlic and allspice to same skillet. Bring mixture to boil, scraping up browned bits. Pour contents of skillet over briskets. Cover tightly with heavy-duty foil. Roast until briskets are very tender, about 2 hours. Uncover; let cool at least 30 minutes.

Transfer briskets to platter. Remove bones from pan and discard. Spoon onions into strainer set over large saucepan. Press onions hard to release juices. Discard onions. Set mushrooms aside. Strain pan juices in roasting pan into same large saucepan. Spoon fat from top. Boil until pan juices coat spoon lightly, 20 minutes. Return mushrooms to sauce. Season to taste with salt and pepper.

Cut briskets diagonally across grain into thin slices; trim fat, if desired. Overlap slices in large casserole. Spoon mushroom sauce over. *(Can be prepared 3 days ahead. Cover with foil and refrigerate. Rewarm covered in 350°F oven 45 minutes.)* Garnish with fresh thyme.

8 SERVINGS

◆ ◆ ◆

This hearty entrée can be prepared several days ahead. Veal brisket is the boned veal breast. If you don't have a roasting pan large enough to hold both briskets, divide the ingredients in half and bake in two pans. If the veal is difficult to find, substitute one 5-pound flat-cut beef brisket and roast until tender, about 3 1/2 hours. Leftovers freeze well.

◆ ◆ ◆

Lamb with Creamy Bean and Rosemary Sauce

◆ ◆ ◆

4   6- to 8-ounce lamb shoulder-blade steaks (about $^3/_4$ inch thick)

$^3/_4$ cup peanut oil

4   teaspoons chopped fresh rosemary or $1^1/_2$ teaspoons dried

2   large garlic cloves, crushed

1   tablespoon olive oil

$^1/_2$ cup minced shallots

3   large garlic cloves, minced

5   tablespoons dry white wine

$1^1/_2$ cups low-salt chicken broth

$1^1/_2$ cups whipping cream

4   fresh rosemary sprigs or 2 teaspoons dried

$^1/_2$ cup frozen lima beans, thawed

$^1/_2$ cup canned pinto beans, rinsed

$^1/_2$ cup canned cannellini (white kidney beans), rinsed

$^1/_2$ cup canned red kidney beans, rinsed

FOR LAMB: Arrange lamb in shallow dish. Combine peanut oil, 4 teaspoons rosemary and 2 garlic cloves. Pour over lamb. Cover and refrigerate overnight, turning occasionally.

FOR SAUCE: Heat olive oil in heavy medium skillet over low heat. Add shallots and 3 garlic cloves and sauté until translucent, about 5 minutes. Increase heat to medium-high; add wine and cook 1 minute. Add broth and boil until reduced to $^1/_2$ cup, about 18 minutes. Add cream and 4 rosemary sprigs and simmer until slightly thickened to sauce consistency, about 8 minutes. Strain sauce and return to skillet. Season to taste with salt and pepper. *(Can be prepared 1 day ahead. Cover and refrigerate.)*

Cook lima beans in small saucepan of boiling salted water until tender, about 4 minutes. Drain. Add to sauce. Add remaining beans to sauce. Warm over medium-low heat.

Preheat broiler. Remove lamb from marinade and season with salt and pepper. Broil lamb about 3 minutes per side for medium-rare.

Divide sauce and beans among 4 plates. Arrange lamb atop.

4 SERVINGS

Crown Roast of Lamb with Shallots, Mustard and Mint

◆ ◆ ◆

3   *tablespoons butter, room temperature*
1   *tablespoon plus ½ teaspoon Dijon mustard*
2   *teaspoons dried rosemary*
1   *crown of lamb made from two 8-rib racks (about 4½ pounds total)*

2   *large shallots, chopped*
1   *cup dry white wine*
¼   *cup chicken stock or canned unsalted broth*
3   *tablespoons chopped fresh mint*

Preheat oven to 450°F. Mix 2 tablespoons butter, 1 tablespoon mustard and 1½ teaspoons rosemary in bowl. Season generously with salt and pepper. Place lamb in roasting pan. Rub all over with butter mixture. Roast 15 minutes. Reduce oven temperature to 350° F. and continue roasting until thermometer inserted into lamb registers 140° F. for medium-rare, about 40 minutes. Transfer lamb to platter; let stand 15 minutes.

Pour off fat from roasting pan and set pan aside. Melt 1 tablespoon butter in heavy large skillet over low heat. Add shallots and ½ teaspoon rosemary; sauté until shallots are tender, about 5 minutes. Add wine to roasting pan and bring to boil over high heat, scraping up any browned bits. Add wine to skillet. Add stock; boil until slightly thickened, about 6 minutes. Mix in ½ teaspoon mustard and mint. Season with salt and pepper.

Carve roast lamb into chops and serve, spooning sauce over.

6 SERVINGS

◆ ◆ ◆

Typically, the crown roast is reserved for special occasions because it offers a spectacular presentation. Be sure to have the butcher assemble the "crown" for you. Offer a watercress salad on the side and pour a dry red wine with the meal.

◆ ◆ ◆

Rosemary-marinated Lamb Chops;
Sautéed Broccoli Rabe with Garlic,
page 124; Steamed Baby Vegetables.

Rosemary-marinated Lamb Chops

◆ ◆ ◆

2   *fresh rosemary bunches*
     Coarse salt
16 *1-inch-thick lamb loin chops*
2   *cups dry white wine*
6   *tablespoons olive oil*
2   *tablespoons red wine vinegar*

Finely chop enough rosemary to measure 2 tablespoons. Rub salt and chopped rosemary all over lamb chops. Divide lamb between 2 glass baking dishes. Pour wine, oil and vinegar over lamb. Season with pepper. Place remaining rosemary sprigs over lamb. Cover and refrigerate at least 2 hours or overnight, turning once.

Preheat oven to 450°F. Remove lamb from marinade and place on baking sheets. Bake about 7 minutes for medium-rare.

Preheat broiler. Transfer lamb to broiler and broil until brown on edges, about 2 minutes per side. Transfer lamb to plates and serve.

8 SERVINGS

◆ ◆ ◆

An easy, do-ahead main course. Offer both a Chianti Classico and a Chardonnay so that diners can choose either a red or a white wine.

◆ ◆ ◆

Lamb Fillet with
Thai Curry Sauce

◆ ◆ ◆

$^1\!/_2$ cup dry white wine

1 tablespoon curry powder

$^3\!/_4$ cup canned coconut milk*

1 tablespoon chopped lemongrass or grated lemon peel

1 large garlic clove, finely chopped

12 Belgian endive leaves, torn into pieces

8 Boston lettuce leaves, torn into pieces

4 radicchio leaves, torn into pieces

2 tablespoons peanut oil

$^1\!/_2$ onion, thinly sliced

1 2- to $2^1\!/_4$-pound rack of lamb, boned, well trimmed

1 zucchini, halved lengthwise, thinly sliced

1 carrot, cut into matchstick-size strips

1 serrano or jalapeño chili, halved, seeded, cut into
    matchstick-size strips

Boil wine and curry in heavy small saucepan 2 minutes. Add coconut milk, lemongrass and garlic. Boil until liquid is reduced to 6 tablespoons, about 10 minutes. Strain, pressing hard on solids. *(Sauce can be prepared 1 day ahead. Cover and refrigerate.)*

Combine Belgian endive, Boston lettuce and radicchio leaves and divide between plates.

Heat oil in heavy large skillet over high heat. Add onion; sauté until golden, about 8 minutes. Push to side of skillet. Season lamb with salt and pepper. Add to skillet; cook 2 minutes per side. Add zucchini and carrot and cook until tender and lamb is rare, stirring occasionally, about 5 minutes. Rewarm sauce. Thinly slice lamb and place atop greens. Spoon sauce over. Garnish with chili.

*Coconut milk is available at Indian, Southeast Asian and Latin American markets.

6 SERVINGS

Black, White and Red Bean Chili with Sausage

◆ ◆ ◆

1 tablespoon olive oil
1¼ pounds Italian sausages (pork or turkey)
1 large onion, cut into ½-inch pieces
1 large red bell pepper, cut into ½-inch pieces
1 large green bell pepper, cut into ½-inch pieces
2 jalapeño chilies, seeded, chopped
1 tablespoon plus 2 teaspoons chili powder
2 teaspoons ground cumin
1½ 28-ounce cans crushed tomatoes in puree
1 15¼-ounce can kidney beans, drained, rinsed
1 15-ounce can cannellini (white kidney beans), drained, rinsed
1 15- to 16-ounce can black beans, drained, rinsed
1 tablespoon balsamic vinegar or red wine vinegar

Sour cream
Chopped fresh cilantro

Heat olive oil in heavy large saucepan over medium-high heat. Add Italian sausages and brown on all sides, turning occasionally, about 8 minutes. Transfer sausages to plate. Add chopped onion to pan and sauté 5 minutes. Add chopped bell peppers and chilies and sauté 1 minute. Add chili powder and cumin and stir until aromatic, about 30 seconds. Add crushed tomatoes and beans. Simmer 15 minutes to blend flavors. Cut sausage into ½-inch pieces. Add to chili and simmer until cooked through, stirring occasionally, about 10 minutes. Mix in vinegar. Season chili to taste with salt and pepper. *(Can be made 2 days ahead. Cover and refrigerate. Before serving, rewarm over medium heat.)*

Spoon chili into bowls. Top with sour cream and cilantro.

4 SERVINGS

Jalapeños, chili powder, cumin and a splash of balsamic vinegar spice up this delicious dish. Offer with a simple mixed green salad and the Fontina, Corn and Jalapeño Quesadillas on page 22.

◆ ◆ ◆

Paprika Pork Patties

◆ ◆ ◆

6 large garlic cloves
¼ pound bacon, diced
6 tablespoons ice water
4 teaspoons sweet Hungarian paprika

1   teaspoon hot Hungarian paprika

³/₄ teaspoon coarse salt

¹/₂ teaspoon black pepper

¹/₂ teaspoon ground allspice

1   pound ground pork

¹/₂ cup chopped drained sauerkraut

With processor running, drop garlic through feed tube and mince. Add next 7 ingredients and process until thick paste forms. Add pork and combine, using on/off turns. Add sauerkraut and just mix in. With moistened hands, shape sausage into six ³/₄-inch-thick patties; arrange on plate.

Heat large nonstick skillet over medium heat. Add sausage patties and cook until brown and just cooked through, about 6 minutes per side. Serve immediately.

6 SERVINGS

Pork Chops with Apple-Corn Bread Stuffing

◆ ◆ ◆

4   ¹/₂-inch-thick boneless pork loin chops, trimmed

1   teaspoon dried thyme

1¹/₂ tablespoons unsalted butter

¹/₂ cup chopped onion

¹/₂ cup chopped peeled tart apple (such as Granny Smith)

³/₄ cup corn bread stuffing mix, crushed

¹/₄ cup water

Preheat oven to 450°F. Season pork with ¹/₂ teaspoon thyme, then salt and pepper. Melt ¹/₂ tablespoon butter in heavy medium skillet over medium-high heat. Add pork chops to skillet; sauté until cooked through, about 3 minutes per side. Transfer pork chops to small baking pan. Melt remaining 1 tablespoon butter in same skillet over medium-high heat. Add chopped onion and apple to skillet and sauté until beginning to soften, about 5 minutes. Add stuffing mix, water and remaining ¹/₂ teaspoon thyme. Stir until water is absorbed and stuffing is moist, about 30 seconds. Mound ¹/₄ of stuffing on each pork chop. Bake until stuffing is crisp and beginning to brown, about 5 minutes.

2 SERVINGS

◆ ◆ ◆

Steamed broccoli spears and red cabbage coleslaw go well with these savory pork chops. For dessert, top vanilla frozen yogurt with warm butterscotch sauce for a lightened version of an old-fashioned sundae.

◆ ◆ ◆

Pork Medallions with Glazed Apples and Cider Sauce

❖ ❖ ❖

2 ½ tablespoons unsalted butter

4 garlic cloves, minced

1 tablespoon dry mustard

2 ½ tablespoons all purpose flour

3 cups chicken stock or canned low-salt broth

3 cups beef stock or canned unsalted broth

2 cups apple cider

8 tablespoons (½ stick) butter

8 large Golden Delicious apples, cored, each cut into 8 wedges

½ cup packed golden brown sugar

2 ¼ pounds pork tenderloins, cut into 1-inch-thick rounds
   All purpose flour

2 tablespoons (¼ stick) butter

½ cup Calvados or applejack

FOR SAUCE: Melt 2½ tablespoons butter in heavy large saucepan over medium heat. Add garlic and mustard and sauté 20 seconds. Add 2½ tablespoons flour and stir 2 minutes. Gradually whisk in stocks and cider. Boil until reduced to sauce consistency, stirring occasionally, about 45 minutes. *(Can be prepared 1 day ahead. Cover and refrigerate.)*

FOR APPLES: Melt 4 tablespoons butter in large skillet over medium-high heat. Add half of apples and half of sugar. Sauté until apples soften, about 5 minutes. Place in bowl. Repeat with 4 tablespoons butter, apples and sugar. Combine all apples in skillet. *(Can be made 4 hours ahead. Keep at room temperature.)*

FOR PORK: Pound pork between sheets of waxed paper to ½-inch thickness. Coat with flour. Melt 2 tablespoons butter in another large skillet over high heat. Add pork in batches; sauté until cooked, about 2 minutes per side. Transfer to plate. Return all pork to skillet. Remove from heat. Add Calvados; ignite with match. When flames subside, return skillet to heat; boil until most liquid evaporates.

Bring sauce to simmer, stirring occasionally. Rewarm apples. Serve pork with apples and cider sauce.

8 SERVINGS

❖ ❖ ❖

This dish is excellent with the Gratin Dauphinois on page 133 and the Green Bean Bundles on page 128. A robust red Burgundy would be a nice complement to the sweet fruit flavors of this main course.

Potée Lorraine

◆ ◆ ◆

6   bacon slices, chopped

3   pounds boneless pork shoulder, cut into 1½-inch cubes

2   medium onions, chopped

2   14½-ounce cans chicken broth

1   14½-ounce can beef broth

1   cup dry white wine

2   bay leaves

1   1½-pound cabbage

3   large carrots, peeled

2   turnips, peeled

2   russet potatoes, peeled

3   15-ounce cans cannellini (white kidney beans), rinsed, drained

¼   teaspoon ground cloves

1   pound green beans, trimmed, cut into 1½-inch pieces

Cook bacon in heavy 8-quart Dutch oven over high heat until fat is rendered, about 4 minutes. Using slotted spoon, transfer bacon to medium bowl. Pour off all but 2 tablespoons fat from pot and reserve. Heat fat in pot over high heat. Working in batches, add pork, sprinkle with salt and pepper and brown lightly on all sides. Transfer each batch to bowl with bacon. Add onions to pot. Reduce heat to medium; cook until tender, about 8 minutes. Return pork and bacon to pot. Add broth, wine and bay leaves. Cover; simmer 1 hour.

Cut cabbage, carrots, turnips and potatoes into ¾- to 1-inch pieces. Heat reserved bacon fat in heavy large skillet over medium-high heat. Add cabbage and cook until wilted, stirring often, about 5 minutes. Add carrots, turnips and potatoes and stir 5 minutes. Add vegetables to pork. Cover and simmer until pork is tender, about 45 minutes.

Add cannellini to stew. Simmer uncovered until stew thickens, stirring occasionally, about 15 minutes. Add cloves. Season to taste with salt and pepper. *(Can be prepared 1 day ahead. Cover and refrigerate. Rewarm over medium heat, stirring frequently.)* Cook green beans in large pot of boiling salted water until crisp-tender, about 5 minutes. Drain and mix into stew. Ladle into shallow bowls and serve.

6 SERVINGS

Traditionally made with beans, bacon, sausage, meat and whatever vegetables are in season, the French "potful" is served in two courses: first the broth, then the rest. This version is presented as a one-dish stew and needs nothing more than bread on the side. Try a salad of roasted fresh beets as an appetizer, and offer an Alsatian Riesling or Gewürztraminer to drink.

◆ ◆ ◆

BISTRO STYLE

When the editorial staff of *Bon Appétit* was asked to come up with the one word that defined "bistro style" for them, the responses were varied. They ranged from "comfortable," "cozy" and "friendly" to "sophisticated," "lively" and "basic." So you can see that even among those in the know, defining what exactly bistro style *is* isn't exactly easy. But knowing it when they see it and tasting it when they eat it — now that's another, simpler thing altogether.

A bistro is a small neighborhood restaurant that serves unpretentious fare in generous portions at reasonable prices to a loyal clientele. The food is fragrant, earthy and seasonal. And while the original bistro is French, the modern version cuts across many cultural and culinary borders.

◆ ◆ ◆

◆ POULTRY ◆

Tarragon-Butter Roast Chicken with Mushroom Sauce

◆ ◆ ◆

1   *6- to 7-pound roasting chicken*
13 *tablespoons Tarragon Butter (see recipe, page 132)*
    Fresh tarragon sprigs

³/₄ *cup dry white wine*
¹/₄ *cup (about) canned chicken broth*

6   *to 8 ounces fresh shiitake or button mushrooms, stemmed, thinly sliced*
6   *large shallots, thinly sliced*
    Minced fresh tarragon

Preheat oven to 450°F. Pat chicken dry. Place in large roasting pan. Slide hand between chicken skin and meat over breast to form pockets. Spread 10 tablespoons Tarragon Butter under skin and over breast meat and over outer skin. Season with salt and pepper. Place 3 tarragon sprigs in cavity. Tie legs together to hold shape. Tuck wings under body.

Roast chicken 15 minutes. Reduce oven temperature to 375°F. Continue roasting until juices run clear when chicken is pierced in thickest part of thigh, basting occasionally with pan juices, about 1 hour 15 minutes. Transfer chicken to platter.

Pour pan juices into glass measuring cup and degrease. Add wine to roasting pan and bring to boil, scraping up any browned bits. Boil 1 minute. Add wine and any drippings from chicken platter to pan juices. Add enough broth to measure 1 cup liquid.

Melt 3 tablespoons Tarragon Butter in heavy large skillet over medium heat. Add mushrooms and shallots and sauté until beginning to soften, about 5 minutes. Add pan juice mixture and boil until beginning to thicken, about 2 minutes. Sprinkle with minced tarragon.

Transfer chicken to platter. Garnish with fresh tarragon sprigs. Slice chicken, spoon mushroom sauce over and serve.

4 SERVINGS

Chicken Saltimbocca

◆ ◆ ◆

8   sun-dried tomatoes (not oil-packed)
1   cup boiling water
2   ounces part skim ricotta cheese
1   egg white
1   teaspoon chopped fresh basil or ½ teaspoon dried
1   teaspoon minced garlic
1   teaspoon minced shallot

4   4-ounce boneless skinless chicken breast halves

    Nonstick vegetable oil spray
1   teaspoon minced shallot
½   cup chicken stock or canned low-salt broth
2   tablespoons skim milk
1   teaspoon grated Parmesan cheese
1   teaspoon minced garlic
1   teaspoon cornstarch dissolved in 1 tablespoon water
3   green onions, finely chopped

1   teaspoon vegetable oil

FOR CHICKEN: Place tomatoes in medium bowl. Pour boiling water over. Let stand until softened, about 30 minutes. Drain well. Finely chop tomatoes. Transfer to medium bowl. Add ricotta, egg white, basil, 1 teaspoon garlic and 1 teaspoon shallot and stir to combine. Set mixture aside.

Using meat mallet or rolling pin, pound chicken breasts between sheets of waxed paper to thickness of ¼ inch. Spread ¼ of cheese mixture over boned side of each breast, leaving ½-inch border. Starting at 1 long side, roll up chicken jelly roll style. Tie with string to secure. *(Can be prepared 2 hours ahead. Cover and refrigerate.)*

FOR SAUCE: Spray heavy small saucepan with nonstick vegetable oil spray. Add 1 teaspoon shallot and sauté 1 minute over medium heat. Add stock, milk, Parmesan and 1 teaspoon garlic. Whisk in cornstarch mixture. Bring to boil, whisking constantly. Cook until thick, about 4 minutes. Mix in onions.

Heat oil in heavy large nonstick skillet over high heat. Add chicken and brown. Reduce heat to medium-high. Cover and cook until chicken is cooked through, turning, about 12 minutes.

Remove strings. Cut each roll into ¾-inch-thick slices. Divide among plates. Bring sauce to simmer. Spoon over chicken.

4 SERVINGS

◆ ◆ ◆

The traditional version of this Italian dish uses veal and prosciutto and has a rich sauce of butter and wine. This is a much lighter rendition.

◆ ◆ ◆

Herbed Chicken Fricassee

◆ ◆ ◆

6   *garlic cloves*
½   *cup plus 2 tablespoons mixed fresh herb leaves (such as marjoram, thyme, sage, rosemary and summer savory)*
2   *tablespoons plus 3 teaspoons olive oil*
2   *tablespoons balsamic vinegar or red wine vinegar*
6   *chicken thighs*
3   *large chicken half breasts, cut crosswise in half*

3   *onions, finely chopped*
1½ *tablespoons all purpose flour*
1   *cup dry white wine*
2   *tablespoons tomato paste*
4   *cups chicken stock or canned low-salt broth*

¼   *cup minced fresh parsley*
     Steamed rice

Finely chop garlic and herbs in processor. Add 2 tablespoons oil and vinegar and blend in. Place chicken thighs and breasts in large baking pan. Spread herb mixture over all sides of chicken. Cover and chill at least 4 hours or overnight.

Scrape herb mixture off chicken and reserve. Season chicken with salt and pepper. Heat 1 teaspoon olive oil in heavy large Dutch oven over medium-high heat. Cook chicken in batches until brown on all sides, turning occasionally and adding remaining 2 teaspoons olive oil as necessary, about 8 minutes. Transfer chicken to baking pan. Add chopped onions to Dutch oven and sauté until tender, about 10 minutes. Sprinkle flour over onions and stir 1 minute. Add 1 cup dry white wine and 2 tablespoons tomato paste and bring to boil, scraping up any browned bits. Boil until liquid is reduced by half, about 3 minutes. Return chicken and herb mixture to Dutch oven. Add 4 cups chicken stock, cover and simmer until chicken is tender, about 20 minutes. *(Can be prepared 2 days ahead. Cover and refrigerate chicken in cooking liquid.)*

Remove chicken from Dutch oven. Boil cooking liquid until reduced to sauce consistency, about 25 minutes. Season to taste with salt and pepper. Return chicken to Dutch oven and heat through. Mix in parsley. Spoon rice onto plates. Top with chicken and sauce.

6 SERVINGS

Herbed Chicken Fricassee; Sautéed Baby Vegetables, page 125; Steamed Rice; Roasted Garlic and Brie Toasts, page 14; Almond Cheesecake Fruit Tart, page 169.

Mustard Chicken with Mixed Greens

♦ ♦ ♦

1   cup olive oil
6   tablespoons white wine vinegar
1   tablespoon plus $^1/_4$ cup Dijon mustard
8   garlic cloves, minced
2   small shallots, minced
$^3/_4$ teaspoon sugar

1   small onion, minced
$^1/_2$ cup dry white wine
$^1/_2$ teaspoon dried thyme, crumbled
8   boneless chicken breast halves

12   cups mixed baby greens

Combine oil, vinegar, 1 tablespoon mustard, 2 minced garlic cloves, shallots and sugar in jar. Season with salt and pepper. Shake to blend. (Dressing can be made 4 days ahead. Refrigerate. Bring to room temperature before using.)

Mix $^1/_4$ cup mustard, remaining 6 minced garlic cloves, onion, wine and thyme in large baking dish. Add chicken to dish; turn to coat. Chill overnight.

Preheat oven to 375°F. Bake chicken until cooked through, about 25 minutes. Transfer chicken to plate and cool. Thinly slice chicken crosswise. (Can be prepared 2 hours ahead.)

In bowl, toss greens with enough dressing to coat. Arrange chicken atop greens. Drizzle more dressing over.

8 SERVINGS

Barbecued Chicken Cheeseburgers

♦ ♦ ♦

♦ ♦ ♦

Two American classics come together for a new crowd pleaser. Peanut butter cookies and fresh nectarines are nice for dessert.

♦ ♦ ♦

$3^1/_2$ pounds ground chicken
$1^1/_3$ cups chopped onion
1   tablespoon (generous) minced fresh thyme or 1 teaspoon dried

2   cups purchased barbecue sauce
12   American or cheddar cheese slices
12   hamburger buns, split, toasted
12   tomato slices
12   lettuce leaves

Line baking sheet with plastic wrap. Mix first 3 ingredients in large bowl. Divide into 12 balls. Flatten each into ½-inch-thick patty. Place on baking sheet. Cover and chill until ready to cook. *(Can be prepared 1 day ahead.)*

Prepare barbecue (medium heat). Place burgers on grill. Cover; grill until cooked through, turning occasionally and brushing with sauce, about 10 minutes. Top with cheese. Cover; cook until cheese melts, 1 minute. Place burgers in buns. Serve, passing remaining sauce, tomatoes and lettuce separately.

12 SERVINGS

Three-Citrus Grilled Chicken

◆ ◆ ◆

⅓	cup fresh orange juice
¼	cup fresh lemon juice
¼	cup olive oil
¼	cup honey
¼	cup frozen lemon juice concentrate, thawed
3	tablespoons fresh lime juice
3	tablespoons chopped fresh mint leaves
1	tablespoon grated orange peel
2	teaspoons grated lemon peel
1¼	teaspoons grated lime peel
¼	teaspoon ground cumin
¼	teaspoon ground cinnamon
⅛	teaspoon salt
⅛	teaspoon ground pepper
4	chicken breast halves with ribs
¼	red onion, thinly sliced

Mix first 14 ingredients in large bowl until blended. Add chicken and onion and turn to coat. Cover and refrigerate at least 2 hours or overnight.

Prepare barbecue (medium heat). Remove chicken from marinade. Pour marinade into heavy small saucepan and bring to boil; remove from heat. Grill chicken until cooked through, basting frequently with marinade and turning occasionally, about 18 minutes. Transfer to plates; serve with marinade.

4 SERVINGS

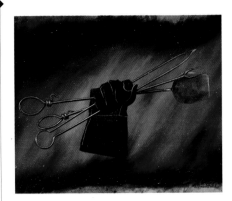

GRILLING TOOLS AND TOYS

While you can certainly get by with little more than a pair of tongs, a few extra tools in your *batterie de barbecue* will make things easier — not to mention a bit more fun.

◆ While tongs make quick work of turning meat, a metal spatula might come in handy, too. A long-handled fork is also useful for this (watch, though, that you don't stab the meat, allowing flavorful juices to run out).

◆ If kebabs are on the menu, a set of good metal skewers with flat shanks (which prevent the meat from spinning around when the skewers are lifted) is useful.

◆ A food thermometer — either the old-fashioned kind that is inserted into the meat prior to cooking or the newer "instant-read" type — is another handy piece of equipment.

◆ A long-handled basting brush is a good idea to have, too.

◆ ◆ ◆

Spinach-stuffed Chicken Breasts

◆ ◆ ◆

1   tablespoon butter
4   ounces mushrooms, finely chopped
1   10-ounce package frozen chopped spinach, thawed,
     squeezed dry
6   ounces cream cheese, room temperature
½   cup chopped fresh chives or green onion tops

6   chicken breast halves
6   tablespoons Dijon mustard

Preheat oven to 450°F. Melt butter in heavy medium skillet over medium heat. Add mushrooms and sauté until tender, about 5 minutes. Cool slightly. Blend spinach, cream cheese and chives in medium bowl. Mix in mushrooms; season with salt and pepper.

Run fingers under skin of each chicken breast to loosen, creating pocket. Spread ⅙ of cheese mixture between skin and meat of each breast. Arrange chicken breasts on baking sheet. Spread 1 tablespoon Dijon mustard over each chicken breast. Bake chicken until golden brown and cooked through, about 20 minutes.

6 SERVINGS

Couscous and Chicken Salad with Orange-Balsamic Dressing

◆ ◆ ◆

4 ½ cups water

3   cups (two 10-ounce boxes) couscous

1   cup dried currants

1   3-pound roasted chicken, skinned, boned, cut into pieces

1 ½ cups diced drained roasted red bell peppers (from jar)

1   15 ½-ounce can chick-peas (garbanzo beans), rinsed, drained

1   cup chopped pitted Kalamata olives*

1   bunch green onions, chopped

½   cup chopped fresh cilantro

¾   cup orange juice

3   tablespoons balsamic vinegar or red wine vinegar

3   tablespoons grated orange peel

1   tablespoon ground cumin

½   cup olive oil
    Romaine lettuce leaves

FOR SALAD: Bring 4 ½ cups water to boil in large saucepan. Add couscous and currants. Cover, remove from heat and let stand 5 minutes. Fluff with fork. Transfer to large bowl and cool.

Mix chicken and next 5 ingredients into cooled couscous.

FOR DRESSING: Mix juice and next 3 ingredients in bowl. Gradually mix in oil. Pour dressing over salad and toss. Season with salt and pepper. *(Can be made 1 day ahead. Cover and chill.)* Line large bowl with romaine. Add salad.

*Black brine-cured Kalamata olives are available at Greek and Italian markets and some supermarkets.

8 SERVINGS

Currants, roasted peppers, chick-peas, olives, green onions and cilantro add color and flavor to this salad. To start, dip wedges of pita bread into store-bought *hummus* (a Middle Eastern chick-pea puree). A slightly chilled Beaujolais or lemonade is a refreshing beverage choice.

◆ ◆ ◆

MADRAS CURRY POWDER

India is known for its many unique spice blends, but surely the most distinctive is curry powder from Madras in the southern part of the country. It has been used in much of the world for centuries, and since the late eighteenth century in the Western world.

Curry powder is a blend of eight cleverly matched, inexpensive spices and herbs: coriander, cumin, turmeric, mustard, fenugreek, red chili, black pepper and curry leaves. Coriander gives the blend its piquant flavor, while cumin and mustard combine to make it spicy. The characteristic golden color and woodsy smell are created by turmeric.

Classically, curry powder is used in sauces for both meat and vegetables, but it can add zip to everything from soups to dips, stuffings to marinades. Try it in the Malaysian Chicken Curry with Peppers here.

◆ ◆ ◆

Malaysian Chicken Curry with Peppers

◆ ◆ ◆

3   tablespoons vegetable oil
1   3- to 3 1/2-pound chicken, cut into 8 pieces
1/2   cup minced shallots (about 4 ounces)
4   teaspoons curry powder
1   medium tomato, finely chopped
1/2   cup coconut milk*
2   teaspoons paprika

2   medium-size red bell peppers, cored, chopped
3   jalapeño chilies, seeded, sliced
2   teaspoons fresh lemon juice

Heat oil in heavy large skillet over medium-high heat. Add chicken and cook until golden on all sides, about 12 minutes. Transfer chicken to plate. Discard all but 1 tablespoon pan drippings. Add shallots to skillet and sauté until slightly softened, about 3 minutes. Add curry powder and stir until aromatic, about 30 seconds. Add tomato, coconut milk and paprika. Season with salt and bring to boil. Return chicken to skillet. Reduce heat to medium-low, cover and cook until chicken is tender, turning chicken and scraping bottom of skillet occasionally, about 25 minutes.

Add peppers, jalapeños and lemon juice to skillet. Cover and cook until peppers are slightly softened, about 5 minutes. Arrange chicken on platter. Degrease pan juices; spoon sauce over chicken.

*Coconut milk is available canned at Indian, Southeast Asian or Latin American markets.

4 SERVINGS

Smoked Chicken, Spinach and Feta Salad

◆ ◆ ◆

1   10-ounce bag fresh spinach leaves
1   bunch bok choy, stems trimmed, leaves sliced
6   ounces smoked chicken, cut into strips
3   bacon slices, cut into 1/2-inch pieces
6   tablespoons Dijon mustard

2   tablespoons red wine vinegar
10 tablespoons olive oil
2   tablespoons water
4   ounces feta cheese, crumbled
    Croutons (optional)

Combine spinach, bok choy and chicken in large bowl. Cook bacon in heavy medium skillet over medium-high heat until crisp. Transfer to paper towels using slotted spoon and drain. Pour off drippings from skillet. Add mustard and vinegar to same skillet and whisk to combine. Whisk in oil and 2 tablespoons water. Add bacon and feta and stir over medium heat just until heated through; do not boil. Add enough dressing to salad to season to taste and toss to coat. Divide among plates. Sprinkle with croutons if desired.

4 SERVINGS

Sautéed Turkey Cutlets with Orange Sauce

◆ ◆ ◆

2   tablespoons all purpose flour
1   pound turkey cutlets (turkey breast slices)
1   tablespoon vegetable oil

$^1/_3$ cup sliced green onions (white part only)
1   large garlic clove, thinly sliced
$^3/_4$ cup fresh orange juice
1   tablespoon low-sodium soy sauce
1   teaspoon oriental sesame oil
$^1/_4$ cup sliced green onion tops

Place flour on sheet of waxed paper; season with salt and pepper. Coat turkey with flour and shake off excess. Heat vegetable oil in heavy large nonstick skillet over high heat. Add turkey in batches; cook until light brown, 2 minutes per side. Transfer turkey to plate.

Reduce heat to medium-high. Add white part of green onions and garlic to skillet and sauté 2 minutes. Add orange juice and soy sauce; boil mixture until slightly thickened, stirring, about 3 minutes. Stir in sesame oil. Season with salt and pepper. Return turkey and any juices to skillet. Simmer just until heated through, 2 minutes. Transfer to plates. Spoon sauce over; sprinkle with green onion tops.

4 SERVINGS

Roast Turkey with
Sausage and Herb Stuffing

◆ ◆ ◆

6   tablespoons (³/₄ stick) unsalted butter, room temperature
1   large shallot, chopped
2   teaspoons chopped fresh thyme or ¹/₂ teaspoon dried
2   teaspoons chopped fresh sage or ¹/₂ teaspoon dried rubbed

1   18- to 20-pound turkey (neck and giblets reserved)
    Sausage and Herb Stuffing (see recipe, page 134)
2   cups chicken stock or canned low-salt broth

1¹/₃ cups dry white vermouth
6   tablespoons all purpose flour
4   cups chicken stock or canned low-salt broth
2   bay leaves
¹/₂ cup chopped fresh parsley

FOR TURKEY: Mix first 4 ingredients in bowl. *(Can be made 1 day ahead. Chill. Bring to room temperature before using.)*

Preheat oven to 400°F. Place turkey in roasting pan. Stuff main turkey cavity with 6 cups stuffing. Spoon remaining stuffing into 8-cup soufflé dish; cover with foil and chill. Rub herb butter over turkey; tie legs together loosely just to hold shape. Place neck, giblets and 2 cups stock around turkey in pan.

Roast turkey 30 minutes. Reduce oven temperature to 350°F; continue roasting until meat thermometer inserted into thickest part of thigh registers 175°F, basting every 30 minutes, about 2¹/₂ hours. Bake stuffing in dish during final 30 minutes of roasting. Transfer turkey to platter; tent with foil and let stand 30 minutes. Continue baking stuffing in dish until hot, about 30 minutes longer.

FOR GRAVY: Pour pan juices into measuring cup. Discard neck and giblets; do not clean pan. Spoon fat from surface of juices and transfer fat to heavy large saucepan; reserve juices. Add 1 cup vermouth to roasting pan; bring to boil, scraping up any browned bits. Boil until reduced to glaze, about 4 minutes. Heat fat in saucepan over medium-high heat. Add flour and whisk until pale golden, about 3 minutes. Gradually whisk in glaze from roasting pan, reserved juices, ¹/₃ cup vermouth, stock and bay leaves. Boil until reduced to sauce consistency, about 20 minutes. Mix in parsley. Season with salt and pepper. Discard bay leaves. Serve with gravy.

12 SERVINGS

Roast Turkey with Sausage and Herb Stuffing; Minted Sugar Snap Peas and Pearl Onions in Brown Butter, page 126; Sweet-Potato Casserole, page 132; Cranberry-Tangerine Relish with Walnuts, page 134.

Turkey Scaloppine with Leeks, Currants and Marsala

◆ ◆ ◆

3   *large leeks (white and pale green parts only), halved lengthwise, sliced (about 6 cups)*
2   *cups chicken stock or canned low-salt broth*
2   *teaspoons sugar*
1   *bay leaf*
1/2   *teaspoon dried thyme, crumbled*
1/4   *teaspoon dried rubbed sage*

1/3   *cup plus 1 tablespoon sweet Marsala*
2   *tablespoons dried currants*

2   *tablespoons long-grain white rice*

1   *pound turkey cutlets*
1/2   *teaspoon minced orange peel (orange part only)*

Fresh sage leaves (optional)
Orange peel strips (optional)

Combine leeks, ⅓ cup chicken stock, sugar, bay leaf, dried thyme and dried sage in heavy large skillet. Season with salt and pepper. Cover and cook over low heat until leeks are very tender, stirring occasionally, about 25 minutes. Uncover and cook until golden brown and liquid evaporates, stirring frequently, about 8 minutes. Discard bay leaf. *(Can be prepared 1 day ahead. Cover and refrigerate. Rewarm before using.)*

Turkey Scaloppine with Currants and Marsala; Roasted Potatoes; Artichoke, Endive and Radicchio Salad with Walnuts, page 140.

Combine ⅓ cup Marsala and currants in bowl. Let stand 30 minutes at room temperature.

Place remaining 1⅔ cups chicken stock in heavy small saucepan. Strain Marsala from currants into stock; reserve currants. Bring stock mixture to boil. Add white rice, reduce heat, cover and simmer until rice is very tender, about 30 minutes. Drain rice; reserve stock mixture. Transfer rice and ¼ cup stock mixture to blender and puree. Add remaining stock mixture to blender and puree until sauce is smooth.

Heat heavy large nonstick skillet over medium-high heat. Season turkey with salt and pepper. Add turkey to skillet and sauté until cooked through and golden brown, about 2 minutes per side. Transfer turkey to plate; tent with foil to keep warm. Add sauce, currants, remaining 1 tablespoon Marsala and minced orange peel to same skillet and bring to boil. Cook until sauce thickens, about 2 minutes.

Spoon leek mixture onto plates. Top with turkey. Spoon sauce over. Garnish with fresh sage leaves and orange peel strips.

4 SERVINGS

Lean turkey replaces the traditional veal in this classic Italian dish. Serve with roasted potatoes flavored with minced orange peel and sage. For dessert, offer coffee frozen yogurt drizzled with *sambuca*, the anise-flavored liqueur from Italy.

Turkey Burgers with Sun-dried Tomato Catsup

◆ ◆ ◆

1   *pound ground turkey breast meat*
½   *cup finely chopped red onion*
¼   *cup finely chopped fresh parsley*
2   *tablespoons plain nonfat yogurt*
2   *tablespoons crumbled soft goat cheese (such as Montrachet)*

4   *sourdough rolls, toasted*
     Sun-dried Tomato Catsup (see recipe, page 136)
     Dill pickle slices

Mix first 4 ingredients in medium bowl. Divide mixture into 4 equal portions; divide each portion in half. Shape into 8 flat patties about 3 inches in diameter. Place ½ tablespoon goat cheese in center of each of 4 patties. Top with remaining patties; pinch edges to seal.

Heat large nonstick skillet over medium-high heat until hot enough to evaporate drop of water on contact. Add burgers; cook 3 minutes. Turn burgers over; cover and cook just until cooked through, 3 minutes longer. Top rolls with burgers, catsup and pickle slices. Serve immediately.

4 SERVINGS

Mushroom and Basil-stuffed Cornish Hens with Mushroom Sauce

◆ ◆ ◆

1	large shallot
½	pound mushrooms, quartered
1	tablespoon unsalted butter
1	tablespoon whipping cream
1	tablespoon Madeira
2	1½-pound Cornish game hens, halved
4	large fresh basil leaves
8	tablespoons (one stick) unsalted butter, chilled, diced
½	cup minced shallots
1	cup hot water
5	tablespoons dry white wine
2	tablespoons whipping cream
½	pound oyster mushrooms, sliced
1	tablespoon chopped fresh tarragon or 1 teaspoon dried
1	teaspoon fresh lemon juice

FOR STUFFING: Finely chop 1 shallot in processor. Add mushrooms and finely chop using on/off turns. Melt butter in heavy large skillet over medium-high heat. Add mushroom mixture and cook until all juices evaporate, stirring often, about 10 minutes. Add 1 tablespoon cream and Madeira and cook over high heat until thick, about 2 minutes. Season with salt and pepper. Cool.

FOR CORNISH HENS: Preheat oven to 400°F. Slide fingertips between skin and meat of breast and leg-thigh portions of hen halves. Spread ¼ of mushroom mixture under loosened skin of each hen half. Place 1 basil leaf under skin to cover stuffing. Season Cornish hens with salt and pepper.

Place ½ tablespoon butter in roasting pan large enough to hold hens. Set in oven until melted. Place hens skin side up in pan. Sprinkle ½ cup shallots around hens; pour 1 cup hot water and wine over. Cover pan tightly with foil. Bake hens until cooked through and tender, about 25 minutes. Transfer hens to broiler pan and keep warm.

Preheat broiler. Strain hen cooking liquid into heavy large skillet. Boil over high heat until reduced to 5 tablespoons, about 5 minutes. Add 2 tablespoons whipping cream, oyster mushrooms and tarragon. Cook until mushrooms are tender and liquid is reduced to glaze, about 8 minutes. Add remaining 7½ tablespoons butter to sauce and stir just until melted. Mix in 1 teaspoon fresh lemon juice. Remove sauce from heat. Season hens to taste with salt and pepper. Broil hens until skin is crisp and brown, about 3 minutes. Arrange hens on platter; spoon sauce over and serve immediately.

4 SERVINGS

Duck with Apples and Figs

◆ ◆ ◆

1   tablespoon vegetable oil
1   5-pound duck
1   onion, chopped
1   carrot, chopped

½   cup Port wine
1   cup canned low-salt chicken broth
½   cup dry red wine
3   figs, quartered
1   teaspoon drained green peppercorns in brine
1   4-inch-long lemon peel strip

4   tablespoons (½ stick) butter
1   large red apple, cored, cut into 8 wedges
1   tablespoon sugar
2   figs, halved

FOR DUCK AND SAUCE: Preheat oven to 400°F. Heat oil in large shallow roasting pan over high heat. Season duck with salt and pepper. Add duck and any neck or giblet pieces to pan. Brown on all sides about 12 minutes. Pour off fat. Arrange onion and carrot around duck. Roast until juices run clear when duck is pierced in thickest part of thigh, about 1 hour. Transfer duck to platter; keep warm.

Pour off fat from pan. Add Port to pan; boil 3 minutes, scraping up browned bits. Transfer mixture to saucepan. Add next 5 ingredients; boil until liquid coats spoon, about 15 minutes.

MEANWHILE, PREPARE GARNISH: Melt 1 tablespoon butter in heavy large skillet over medium-high heat. Add apple; sprinkle with sugar. Cook 10 minutes, turning once. Add figs; sauté 2 minutes.

Strain sauce into another saucepan, pressing hard; reheat. Whisk in 3 tablespoons butter. Season with salt and pepper. Remove breasts and legs from duck. Slice meat. Arrange on plates. Garnish with apples and figs. Spoon sauce over duck.

2 TO 4 SERVINGS

◆ ◆ ◆

OUTDOOR BARBECUE FOR EIGHT

MIXED GRILL OF SHRIMP, SAUSAGE
AND MUSHROOMS, PAGE 95

PEPPERY GRILLED GARLIC BREAD,
PAGE 156

MIXED GREEN SALAD

RIESLING

ICE CREAM SUNDAES WITH
CHOCOLATE SAUCE

◆ ◆ ◆

The braising liquid in this dish is reduced to a savory glaze that is used as a sauce for the fish. Accompany it with the Stir-fried Vegetables with Garlic and Ginger on page 124 and steamed rice spiked with dried crushed red pepper. A good beverage choice is chilled light beer or iced tea. Finish with refreshing pineapple sorbet garnished with mint.

◆ ◆ ◆

Oriental Braised Fish with Bok Choy

◆ ◆ ◆

1	cup sake
1/2	cup fish stock or bottled clam juice
1 1/2	tablespoons minced peeled fresh ginger
1 1/2	tablespoons minced garlic
1	tablespoon low-sodium soy sauce
1/4	teaspoon chili oil*
4	4-ounce orange roughy or sea bass fillets
1	medium bok choy (about 18 ounces), bottom 4 inches cut off and discarded
1	teaspoon minced fresh cilantro

Bring first 6 ingredients to simmer in heavy large nonstick skillet. Add fish, cover and simmer until fish is cooked through, turning once, about 5 minutes. Transfer fish to plate using slotted spatula; tent with foil to keep warm. Add bok choy to cooking liquid, cover and simmer until just tender, about 4 minutes. Using tongs, transfer bok choy to plates. Tent with foil to keep warm. Boil liquid in skillet until reduced to 1/4 cup, about 6 minutes. Mix cilantro and any accumulated juices from fish into sauce. Place fish atop bok choy, allowing dark green leaves to show. Spoon sauce over fish and serve.

*Available at Asian markets and in many supermarkets.

4 SERVINGS

Roast Halibut with Gingered Vegetables

◆ ◆ ◆

4	6-ounce halibut fillets (about 1 inch thick)
2	teaspoons hazelnut oil or olive oil
3/4	cup thinly sliced onion
1	tablespoon minced peeled fresh ginger
1/2	teaspoon five-spice powder
1/2	cup matchstick-size carrot strips
1/2	cup thinly sliced red bell pepper

$^1/_2$ cup thinly sliced green bell pepper

1 tablespoon (or more) water

3 tablespoons chopped fresh cilantro

$^1/_3$ cup chopped green onions

3 tablespoons pine nuts, toasted

2 tablespoons minced jalapeño chilies

$^1/_2$ cup fish stock or clam juice

1 tablespoon low-sodium soy sauce

Heat large nonstick skillet over medium-high heat. Season halibut with salt and pepper. Add to skillet; cook just until cooked through, about 4 minutes per side. Transfer to platter; cover with foil and keep warm.

Heat 1 teaspoon hazelnut oil in same skillet; add onion, ginger and five-spice powder and sauté 3 minutes. Add carrot, bell peppers and 1 tablespoon water and cook until crisp-tender, adding more water if vegetables stick, about 4 minutes. Stir in 2 tablespoons cilantro. Keep warm.

Heat remaining 1 teaspoon hazelnut oil in heavy small skillet over medium-high heat. Add green onions, pine nuts and jalapeños and stir 2 minutes. Mix in fish stock and soy sauce; boil until liquid is slightly reduced, about 3 minutes. Season with salt and pepper.

Arrange vegetables on platter. Place halibut fillets over. Pour sauce over fish and sprinkle with remaining cilantro.

4 SERVINGS

Roast Halibut with Gingered Vegetables.

Swordfish with Onions, Red Peppers and Lemon-Saffron Sauce

◆ ◆ ◆

◆ ◆ ◆

Accompany this light entrée with steamed green beans and new potatoes. Pour a chilled Chardonnay.

◆ ◆ ◆

4   green onions, white and green parts chopped separately
½   cup dry white wine
¼   cup fish stock or bottled clam juice
¼   teaspoon (scant) saffron threads

4   8-ounce swordfish steaks, about ¾ inch thick
3   tablespoons fresh lemon juice
5   teaspoons olive oil
2   garlic cloves, minced

2   small red bell peppers, cut into ¼-inch-wide strips

¼   cup (½ stick) chilled unsalted butter, cut into pieces
     Lemon wedges

Combine white part of green onions, dry white wine, fish stock and saffron threads in heavy small saucepan. Boil sauce over medium-high heat until reduced to ½ cup, about 7 minutes. *(Sauce can be prepared 1 day ahead. Cover tightly and refrigerate.)*

Place fish in single layer in large glass baking dish. Pour lemon juice and 2 teaspoons oil over fish. Sprinkle with garlic. Turn fish to coat. Let stand 15 minutes at room temperature.

Heat 1 teaspoon oil in heavy medium nonstick skillet over medium heat. Add bell peppers and sauté until tender, about 8 minutes.

Heat remaining 2 teaspoons oil in heavy large skillet over medium-high heat. Add fish to skillet, reserving marinade in dish. Cook fish just until cooked through, about 3 minutes per side.

Rewarm bell peppers and divide among plates. Top with fish. Add sauce and any remaining marinade to fish cooking skillet and bring to boil. Remove from heat. Add butter and whisk just until melted. Spoon sauce over fish. Sprinkle with green part of onion. Garnish with lemon wedges.

4 SERVINGS

Swordfish with Two-Squash, Potato and Tomato Sauté

♦ ♦ ♦

4   1-inch-thick swordfish steaks, about 8 ounces each
2   tablespoons Dijon or coarse-grained mustard
2   tablespoons fresh lime juice
½   cup olive oil
2   shallots, chopped
2   tablespoons chopped fresh rosemary or 1½ teaspoons dried

1   pound baby red potatoes

3   tablespoons olive oil
3   large shallots, minced
2   tablespoons minced fresh rosemary or 1½ teaspoons dried
2   zucchini squash, sliced
2   yellow crookneck squash, sliced
1   basket cherry tomatoes, stemmed

     Fresh rosemary sprigs (optional)

FOR FISH: Place fish in glass baking dish. Combine mustard and lime juice in small bowl. Gradually whisk in ½ cup oil. Add 2 shallots, 2 tablespoons rosemary and generous amount of pepper. Spoon marinade over fish, turning to coat. Let stand at room temperature 30 minutes or refrigerate up to 3 hours.

FOR VEGETABLES: Cook potatoes in large pot of boiling water until just tender. Drain. Cool. Slice potatoes. *(Can be prepared 3 hours ahead. Cover and chill.)*

Prepare barbecue (medium-high heat) or preheat broiler. Sprinkle fish with salt. Without removing marinade, grill fish until just cooked through, about 4 minutes per side. Place fish on platter.

Meanwhile, heat 3 tablespoons oil in large skillet over medium heat. Add 3 shallots and 2 tablespoons rosemary; cook until shallots are tender, about 5 minutes. Add all squash; sauté until crisp-tender, about 8 minutes. Add potatoes and tomatoes; stir until heated through. Season with salt and pepper.

Spoon vegetables around fish. Garnish with rosemary sprigs, if desired. Serve immediately.

4 SERVINGS

Swordfish with Mustard-Basil Butter

◆ ◆ ◆

$^{1}/_{4}$ cup ($^{1}/_{2}$ stick) unsalted butter, room temperature
2   tablespoons Dijon mustard
2   tablespoons finely chopped fresh basil

   Vegetable oil
4   8-ounce swordfish steaks, $^{3}/_{4}$ inch thick
   Fresh basil sprigs

Mix first 3 ingredients in small bowl.

Prepare barbecue or preheat broiler. Brush grill with vegetable oil. Season fish with salt and pepper. Grill fish just until cooked through, about 3 minutes per side. Transfer to plates. Top each with spoonful of mustard-basil butter. Garnish with basil sprigs and serve.

4 SERVINGS

◆ ◆ ◆

Serve these sandwiches with the Potato, Beet and Cucumber Salad on page 143. Fresh strawberries and cookies from the bakery round out the meal nicely. Pour a dry white wine or iced tea.

◆ ◆ ◆

Smoked Salmon and Goat Cheese Sandwiches

◆ ◆ ◆

$^{1}/_{2}$ pound soft mild goat cheese, room temperature
10 tablespoons minced fresh arugula or watercress
5   tablespoons olive oil
6   teaspoons minced fresh chives
1   pound smoked salmon slices
2   tablespoons fresh lemon juice

12 $^{1}/_{2}$-inch-thick egg bread slices
   Fresh arugula or watercress leaves
12 thin lemon slices

Mix cheese, 6 tablespoons arugula, 2 tablespoons oil and 2 teaspoons chives in bowl. Season with pepper. Arrange salmon in single layer on large plate. Drizzle 3 tablespoons oil over. Spoon lemon juice over. Sprinkle with 4 tablespoons minced arugula, 4 teaspoons chives and pepper. *(Can be prepared 4 hours ahead.)*

Just before serving, toast bread. Spread with goat cheese mixture; top with salmon. Place sandwiches on plates. Tuck arugula under sandwiches. Make cut in each lemon slice from center to edge. Twist 1 slice atop each sandwich.

4 SERVINGS

You can use only wild mushrooms in the ragout, or pair them with some button mushrooms if you prefer. Start out with a bowl of steamed clams, then accompany the salmon with new potatoes and green beans. Pour a dry white wine, such as a Pinot Blanc.

◆ ◆ ◆

Grilled Trout with Herbs; Lemon Caesar Salad, page 142; Sliced Tomatoes and Mozzarella.

Salmon Fillets with Wild Mushroom Ragout

◆ ◆ ◆

3   *tablespoons butter*
5   *shallots, minced*
18 *ounces mixed mushrooms (such as oyster, chanterelle, morel)*
³⁄₄ *cup bottled clam juice*
³⁄₄ *cup dry white wine*
3   *tablespoons whipping cream*
2   *teaspoons chopped fresh tarragon or ¹⁄₂ teaspoon dried*

6   *6- to 8-ounce salmon fillets*
    Fresh lemon juice
2   *tablespoons butter, melted*
    Fresh tarragon sprigs

Melt 3 tablespoons butter in heavy large skillet over medium heat. Add shallots and sauté 2 minutes. Increase heat to medium-high. Add mushrooms; sauté until beginning to brown, about 8 minutes. Add clam juice and wine; boil until liquids are syrupy and almost evaporated, about 20 minutes. *(Can be made 6 hours ahead. Cover and chill. Rewarm over medium heat, stirring frequently.)* Add cream to mushrooms; boil until thickened, about 1 minute. Mix in chopped tarragon. Season with salt and pepper.

Preheat broiler. Arrange salmon skin side down on broiler pan. Brush with lemon juice, then butter. Sprinkle with salt and pepper. Broil until just cooked through, without turning, about 6 minutes. Transfer to plates. Spoon mushrooms over. Garnish with tarragon.

6 SERVINGS

Grilled Trout with Herbs

◆ ◆ ◆

12 *fresh rosemary sprigs*
12 *fresh oregano sprigs*
12 *fresh parsley sprigs*
6   *whole trout*
³⁄₄ *cup olive oil*
¹⁄₂ *cup plus 1 tablespoon fresh lemon juice*

Place herbs inside trout, dividing evenly. Arrange trout in single layer in glass baking dish. Whisk oil and lemon juice together. Pour over trout. Cover and refrigerate 2 hours, turning once.

Prepare barbecue (medium-high heat). Remove trout from marinade. Pour marinade into heavy small saucepan. Grill trout until cooked though, about 15 minutes, turning once. Transfer to platter. Bring marinade to boil. Spoon over trout and serve.

6 SERVINGS

Broiled Fish with Black-Bean Salsa

◆ ◆ ◆

1 15- to 16-ounce can black beans, rinsed, drained
2 oranges, peel and white pith removed, chopped
1 tomato, seeded, chopped
½ cup chopped fresh cilantro
1 large jalapeño chili, seeded but not deveined, minced
1½ tablespoons fresh lime juice
1 tablespoon olive oil
1 avocado, peeled, pitted, chopped

4 6-ounce grouper or red snapper fillets
  Olive oil
  Fresh lime juice
  Chopped fresh cilantro

Combine first 7 ingredients in medium bowl. Season salsa to taste with salt and pepper. *(Can be prepared 1 day ahead. Cover and refrigerate.)* Mix chopped avocado into salsa.

Preheat broiler. Brush fish with oil; sprinkle with fresh lime juice, salt and pepper. Broil without turning until just cooked through, about 9 minutes per inch of thickness. Transfer fish to plates. Sprinkle with chopped fresh cilantro. Serve fish with salsa.

4 SERVINGS

THE WHOLE FISH STORY

There's something wonderfully indulgent about serving a whole small fish to each guest, and it isn't as difficult as you might think. It's especially easy with trout, since there is no need to scale them, and they're very easy to bone. Here's a simple way to serve a whole fish.

◆ Grill the fish, then place it on a flat surface, such as a wooden chopping block. Using a small knife, cut through the skin along the backbone, working from head to tail. If desired, carefully loosen the skin from the cut edge and peel off. Using a spatula or fork, loosen the fillet from the bone and lift off; when properly cooked, the fillet should separate easily from the bone. Then lift the exposed bone from the underlying fillet. Discard head and tail with bones.

◆ ◆ ◆

Clams with White Beans and Tomato Sauce

◆ ◆ ◆

1¹/₄ cups dried Great Northern white beans

4   cups water
2   onions, halved
6   garlic cloves, sliced
1   cup olive oil

2   pounds tomatoes, quartered
1   large onion, coarsely chopped
1   large red bell pepper, cut into 1-inch pieces
1   cup dry white wine
4   garlic cloves
1   teaspoon sugar
2¹/₂ pounds small clams, scrubbed

Place white beans in medium bowl. Cover with water. Let white beans soak overnight.

Combine 4 cups water, 2 onions, 6 garlic cloves and ¹/₂ cup olive oil in large pot. Drain white beans and add to pot. Simmer until beans are tender, stirring occasionally, about 1 hour. Drain beans, discarding onions.

Working in batches, puree tomatoes, chopped onion, bell pepper, dry white wine, 4 garlic cloves, sugar and remaining ½ cup olive oil in food processor. Transfer tomato mixture to heavy large skillet. Simmer until thick and saucelike, stirring occasionally, about 30 minutes. Season sauce to taste with salt and pepper. Add clams, cover and cook until clams open, about 8 minutes. Discard any clams that do not open. Add beans to sauce and bring to boil. Divide among soup bowls and serve.

6 SERVINGS

Shellfish Ragout

◆ ◆ ◆

2	tablespoons olive oil
1	large onion, thinly sliced
1	large fennel bulb, trimmed, sliced
2	large garlic cloves, minced
1	teaspoon fennel seeds
3	8-ounce bottles clam juice
1	28-ounce can Italian plum tomatoes
½	cup dry white wine
½	teaspoon saffron threads

3	pounds small clams or mussels, scrubbed
1	pound uncooked medium shrimp, peeled, deveined
1	pound bay scallops

Heat oil in heavy large Dutch oven over medium-high heat. Add onion and sliced fennel and sauté until tender, about 15 minutes. Add garlic and fennel seeds and sauté 3 minutes. Add clam juice, tomatoes with juices and wine. Bring to boil, breaking up tomatoes with spoon. Add saffron, reduce heat and simmer until liquid thickens slightly, about 35 minutes. *(Can be made 1 day ahead. Cover and chill. Bring to simmer before continuing.)*

Add clams to broth, cover and simmer until clams open, about 6 minutes. Add shrimp and scallops; simmer until shrimp are pink and scallops are opaque, about 3 minutes. Serve immediately.

6 SERVINGS

◆ ◆ ◆

Clams or mussels, shrimp and scallops star in this fennel- and saffron-flavored stew. Pour a Pinot Grigio or another full-bodied dry white wine during the meal.

◆ ◆ ◆

Szechuan peppercorns are familiar to anyone who frequents Chinese or Thai restaurants. But as an ingredient, they remain puzzling. To begin with, the Szechuan peppercorn is not a peppercorn. It's called the flower pepper or the anise pepper, though it's not a flower either, and it doesn't taste anything like anise. And while it does have a distinctive aroma, it's hard to pin down just what it does smell of; that, and it has no real identifiable taste — it's prized more for the tingling sensation it leaves in the mouth.

To be sure, Szechuan peppercorns do come from Szechuan, the vast central province of China that is famed for its spicy contributions to the country's cuisine. They are the reddish-brown berries of the prickly ash tree, which grows throughout China.

◆ ◆ ◆

Scandinavian Open-Face Bay Shrimp Sandwiches

◆ ◆ ◆

$1/2$	cup mayonnaise
$1/2$	cup chopped fresh dill
4	teaspoons Dijon mustard
2	teaspoons fresh lemon juice
4	egg or pumpernickel bread slices, toasted
1	pound cooked bay shrimp, drained, patted dry
4	butter lettuce leaves
$1/2$	English hothouse cucumber, thinly sliced
4	tomato wedges
4	thin lemon slices
4	fresh dill sprigs

Combine first 4 ingredients in medium bowl. Season with salt and pepper. Spread 1 tablespoon dressing over each bread slice. Mix shrimp into remaining dressing. Place 1 lettuce leaf on each bread slice, pressing to adhere. Arrange 6 cucumber slices atop lettuce on each slice. Arrange shrimp mixture atop cucumbers. Garnish each sandwich with tomato wedge, lemon slice and dill sprig.

4 SERVINGS

Seared Scallops and Asparagus with Asian Cream Sauce

◆ ◆ ◆

$3 1/2$	teaspoons Szechuan peppercorns
$3/4$	cup sake
$1/3$	cup finely chopped shallots
$1/3$	cup finely chopped fresh ginger
3	tablespoons rice vinegar
$1/2$	cup whipping cream
12	asparagus spears, trimmed to 4-inch lengths
10	large sea scallops
1	tablespoon unsalted butter
1	tablespoon chopped fresh chives

Finely chop peppercorns in processor. Cook sake, shallots, ginger, vinegar and $^1/_2$ teaspoon chopped peppercorns in small saucepan over medium heat until liquid is reduced to 2 tablespoons, about 15 minutes. Add cream; simmer until liquid coats spoon, about 6 minutes. Strain into another small saucepan.

Cook asparagus in saucepan of boiling salted water 2 minutes. Drain. Refresh under cold water; drain. Sprinkle remaining chopped peppercorns over both sides of scallops. Season with salt.

Melt butter in large nonstick skillet over high heat. Add scallops; cook until golden and almost cooked through, turning occasionally, about 4 minutes. Add asparagus; sauté until scallops are cooked through and asparagus is hot, about 30 seconds. Arrange scallops on plates. Bring sauce to simmer. Spoon sauce around scallops. Garnish with asparagus. Sprinkle with chives.

2 SERVINGS

Shrimp and Endive Salad with Tomato Dressing

◆ ◆ ◆

$^3/_4$ *pound coarsely chopped plum tomatoes*
$^1/_2$ *cup olive oil*
5 *tablespoons balsamic vinegar or 3 tablespoons red wine vinegar*
1 *small garlic clove*

4 *heads Belgian endive, thinly sliced lengthwise*
2 *tablespoons olive oil*
12 *large peeled deveined cooked shrimp*
$^1/_2$ *cup sliced fresh basil leaves*

Puree first 4 ingredients in blender until smooth. Pour into bowl. Season dressing to taste with salt and pepper. *(Can be prepared 1 day ahead. Refrigerate. Bring to room temperature before using.)*

Toss endive with 2 tablespoons oil in large bowl. Season to taste with salt and pepper. Spoon dressing onto plates. Mound endive in center. Arrange shrimp around endive. Sprinkle with basil.

2 SERVINGS

Tournedos of Scallops with Crispy Noodles and Curry Vinaigrette

◆ ◆ ◆

3   ounces dried Chinese egg noodles
    Olive oil

1   large leek
16 large sea scallops, connective muscle removed
8   6-inch wooden skewers
    Olive oil

1   tablespoon olive oil

    Curry Vinaigrette (see recipe, page 137)

FOR NOODLES: Cook egg noodles in pot of boiling salted water just until tender, 4 minutes. Drain. Refresh under cold water; drain completely. Transfer to bowl. Drizzle with olive oil and toss. *(Can be prepared 1 day ahead.)*

FOR SCALLOPS: Bring pot of water to boil. Peel off 4 outer leaves from leek (reserve remaining leek for another use). Add leaves to pot and cook until wilted, about 30 seconds. Drain. Refresh under cold water. Drain; pat dry. Trim leaves to 1-inch width. On work surface place 4 scallops in circle, edges touching. Wrap 1 leek leaf around scallops. Skewer scallop package and leek with 2 skewers in

◆ ◆ ◆

A clever, impressive presentation in which the scallops are "tied" with a cooked leek strip.

◆ ◆ ◆

crisscross pattern. Repeat with remaining scallops, leek leaves and skewers. Brush with olive oil. Season with salt and pepper.

Heat 1 tablespoon oil in large nonstick skillet over medium heat. Form noodles into four 4-inch patties. Add to skillet; season with salt and pepper. Cook until crisp, about 6 minutes per side. Place on plates; keep warm.

Heat large nonstick skillet over high heat. Add scallop packages and cook until scallops are springy to touch, about 3 minutes per side. Top each noodle patty with 1 scallop package. Remove skewers. Drizzle vinaigrette over scallops and serve immediately.

4 SERVINGS

Mixed Grill of Shrimp, Sausage and Mushrooms

◆ ◆ ◆

3/4   cup olive oil
2   tablespoons fresh thyme leaves or 1 tablespoon dried
2   large garlic cloves, minced
1/2   teaspoon dried crushed red pepper
32   large uncooked shrimp, peeled, deveined

32   crimini or button mushrooms, stems trimmed
8   bamboo skewers, soaked 30 minutes in water
1 1/2 pounds andouille sausage or other spicy smoked fully
       cooked sausage, cut into 3/4-inch-thick rounds

Blend olive oil, thyme, minced garlic and crushed red pepper in processor 1 minute. Pour mixture into large bowl. Add shrimp and let stand 1 hour at room temperature.

Remove shrimp from marinade; reserve marinade. Thread 1 mushroom horizontally on 1 skewer. Hold 1 andouille piece in curve of 1 shrimp; thread together on skewer, sliding next to mushroom. Repeat, alternating a total of 4 mushrooms, 4 shrimp and 4 andouille pieces on each skewer. *(Can be prepared 1 day ahead. Cover and chill reserved marinade and skewers separately.)*

Prepare barbecue (medium-high heat). Bring reserved marinade to boil in heavy small saucepan. Arrange skewers on grill and brush with marinade. Grill until shrimp are cooked through, turning occasionally and basting with marinade, about 8 minutes. Transfer to plates and serve immediately.

8 SERVINGS

◆ ◆ ◆

In this terrific recipe, the shish kebab meets the mixed grill. Skewers of fiery *andouille* sausage, sweet shrimp and woodsy mushrooms basted with a fragrant herb oil make a colorful and tasty entrée. For an even smokier flavor, soak mesquite chips for one hour in water, then drain and add to the fire. Offer a green salad alongside and pour a chilled Riesling.

◆ ◆ ◆

◆ ◆ ◆

LAZY-DAY BRUNCH

◆ ◆ ◆

Sweet Potatoes Topped with Vegetarian Black Bean Chili

◆ ◆ ◆

4   *large sweet potatoes*

1   *tablespoon olive oil*
2   *cups diced red bell pepper*
1½   *cups chopped onions*
1   *tablespoon minced garlic*
1   *tablespoon chili powder*
2   *teaspoons ground cumin*
1   *14½- to 16-ounce can ready-cut peeled tomatoes with juices*
1   *15- to 16-ounce can black beans, rinsed thoroughly, drained*
2   *cups diced yellow crookneck squash*
1   *tablespoon minced seeded jalapeño chili*

4   *lime wedges*
     Plain nonfat yogurt (optional)
     Chopped fresh cilantro (optional)

◆ ◆ ◆

Anyone who thinks meatless cooking means leaving the table hungry will love this satisfying combination. It's a one-dish meal on its own, with great texture and terrific flavor, too.

◆ ◆ ◆

Preheat oven to 400°F. Place sweet potatoes in baking dish. Pierce with fork and bake until tender, about 1 hour 15 minutes.

Meanwhile, heat olive oil in large nonstick skillet over medium-low heat. Add diced bell pepper and chopped onions and sauté until golden, about 10 minutes. Add minced garlic and stir mixture 2 minutes. Stir in chili powder and ground cumin, then tomatoes and beans and bring mixture to simmer. Reduce heat to low, cover and cook 20 minutes. *(Chili can be prepared 1 day ahead. Cover and refrigerate. Rewarm over low heat before continuing.)* Add diced yellow squash and minced jalapeño; cover chili and cook until squash is crisp-tender, about 6 minutes.

Arrange 1 sweet potato on each of 4 plates. Split potatoes open; mash slightly. Spoon some chili into center of each. Squeeze lime juice over. Top with yogurt and chopped cilantro, if desired. Pass remaining chili separately.

4 SERVINGS

Practically Nonfat Bean and Green Risotto

◆ ◆ ◆

2   14 ¹/₂-ounce cans vegetable broth
1   cup dry white wine
1   large onion, chopped
1   large leek (white and pale green parts), chopped
1   cup medium-grain white rice
2   large garlic cloves, chopped

1   15- to 16-ounce can red beans or kidney beans, rinsed, drained
1   large head radicchio or ¹/₄ head curly endive, thinly sliced
2   arugula bunches, thinly sliced or 1 cup sliced curly endive
    Grated Parmesan cheese (optional)

Bring broth and wine to boil in heavy large saucepan. Add onion, leek, rice and garlic and bring to boil. Reduce heat to medium-low and simmer uncovered until rice is tender and mixture is thick and creamy, stirring occasionally, about 30 minutes.

Mix beans, radicchio and arugula into rice and cook until vegetables wilt, about 2 minutes. Season to taste with salt and pepper. Serve, passing Parmesan separately if desired.

MAKES ABOUT 5 CUPS

◆ ◆ ◆

Sophisticated and satisfying, this can be offered as a meatless main course or as a hearty side dish.

◆ ◆ ◆

Leek and Cheese Blintzes with Tomato Coulis

◆ ◆ ◆

2   tablespoons (¹/₄ stick) unsalted butter
5   cups thinly sliced leeks (white and pale green parts only)
4   garlic cloves, minced
1   teaspoon chopped fresh thyme or ¹/₂ teaspoon dried
2   cups whole milk ricotta cheese
1   cup grated Parmesan cheese (about 3 ounces)
2   large egg yolks

12   Basic Crepes (see recipe, page 179)

2   tablespoons olive oil
¹/₂ cup chopped shallots
4   garlic cloves, chopped
1   pound plum tomatoes, chopped
1   cup vegetable broth
¹/₄ cup dry white wine
1   bay leaf

4   tablespoons (about) unsalted butter

     Fresh thyme sprigs

FOR FILLING: Melt 2 tablespoons butter in heavy large skillet over medium-low heat. Add leeks, 4 garlic cloves and thyme and sauté until leeks are very tender and golden brown, about 20 minutes. Transfer mixture to bowl and cool. Mix in both cheeses. Season to taste with salt and pepper. Mix in egg yolks.

Line baking sheet with foil. Divide filling among crepes, mounding slightly in center. Fold 1 side of crepe over filling and press gently to flatten. Fold opposite side over. Fold remaining 2 sides in, enclosing filling and forming packet. Place seam side down on foil-lined sheet. Repeat with remaining crepes. *(Can be prepared 1 day ahead. Cover and chill.)*

FOR COULIS: Heat olive oil in heavy medium saucepan over medium-low heat. Add chopped shallots and 4 garlic cloves and sauté until tender, about 5 minutes. Mix in tomatoes, broth, white wine and bay leaf. Simmer until tomatoes are very tender, stirring occasionally, about 30 minutes. Discard bay leaf. Puree mixture in blender. Return puree to saucepan and boil until reduced to 2 cups, about 7 minutes. Season coulis to taste with salt and pepper. *(Can be prepared 6 hours ahead. Cover and let stand at room temperature.)*

◆ ◆ ◆

A sophisticated brunch dish with components that can be made ahead of time. You'll find the Basic Crepes recipe on page 179. Begin with the Springtime Mimosas on page 39; round out the main course with the Sesame Asparagus on page 125.

◆ ◆ ◆

Preheat oven to 250°F. Melt 1 tablespoon unsalted butter in heavy large skillet over medium-low heat. Working in batches, place blintzes seam side down in skillet and cook until golden brown, turning once and adding more butter to skillet as necessary, about 5 minutes. Transfer to baking sheet; place in oven to keep warm.

Bring coulis to simmer. Arrange blintzes on platter. Garnish with thyme sprigs. Serve, passing coulis separately.

MAKES 12

Green Corn Tamales

◆ ◆ ◆

12   ears yellow corn
3   cups yellow cornmeal

$^1/_4$ cup solid vegetable shortening
$^1/_4$ cup ($^1/_2$ stick) unsalted butter, room temperature
$^1/_4$ cup plus 2 tablespoons sugar
$^1/_4$ cup half and half
$1^1/_2$ teaspoons salt

6   ounces cheddar cheese, cut into twelve $^1/_2$ x $^1/_2$ x 3-inch strips
2   7-ounce cans whole mild green chilies, cut into $1^1/_2$ x 3-inch strips

Remove husks from corn and reserve. Cut kernels off cobs. Combine 8 cups corn kernels (reserve remainder for another use) and $1^1/_2$ cups cornmeal in food processor. Grind to chunky puree.

Using electric mixer, beat shortening and butter in large bowl until creamy. Mix in sugar, half and half and salt. Add corn puree and remaining $1^1/_2$ cups cornmeal; mix to combine.

Overlap 2 corn husk pieces on work surface. Spread $^1/_4$ cup corn filling down center of husks, forming 2 x 4-inch rectangle. Place 1 cheese strip and 2 chili strips in center of filling. Spread $^1/_4$ cup filling over chili and cheese, covering completely. Fold 2 long sides of husks over filling; fold in ends. Tie with string. Repeat with remaining husks, filling, cheese and chilies, forming 12 tamales.

Stand tamales on steamer rack. Place rack over boiling water. Cover and steam until tamales are firm to touch, about 50 minutes. *(Tamales can be prepared 1 day ahead. Cover tightly and refrigerate. Resteam over boiling water until hot, about 20 minutes.)*

MAKES 12

Spicy Tofu and Vegetable Stir-fry with Soba Noodles

◆ ◆ ◆

1 *ounce dried shiitake mushrooms*
2 *cups hot water*
1 *14-ounce package firm Chinese tofu*

1 *tablespoon plus 1 teaspoon cornstarch*
2 *teaspoons chili paste with garlic*
2 *tablespoons light soy sauce*

8 *ounces buckwheat soba noodles or linguine*
2 *tablespoons oriental sesame oil*

2 *tablespoons vegetable oil*
1 *green onion bunch, chopped*
2 *tablespoons minced peeled fresh ginger*
6 *large bok choy leaves, cut crosswise into ¼-inch-thick slices*
5 *ounces snow peas, trimmed*

Place mushrooms in bowl. Cover with 2 cups hot water and let stand until softened, about 30 minutes. Drain tofu on paper towels 20 minutes. Cut tofu into ¾-inch pieces and drain on paper towels.

Drain mushrooms, reserving soaking liquid. Squeeze liquid from mushrooms, then slice, discarding stems. Pour 1 cup soaking liquid into small cup. Mix in cornstarch. Combine remaining soaking liquid, chili paste with garlic and soy sauce in another cup.

Cook soba in large pot of boiling salted water until just tender but still firm to bite. Drain well. Toss with 1 tablespoon sesame oil.

Meanwhile, heat vegetable oil in wok or heavy large skillet over high heat. Add chopped green onions and fresh ginger and stir until aromatic, about 30 seconds. Add bok choy and stir 2 minutes. Add mushrooms and snow peas and stir to coat with oil. Sprinkle with salt. Add chili paste mixture. Cover and boil until vegetables are just crisp-tender, about 1 minute. Uncover, add tofu and simmer until heated through. Stir cornstarch mixture to combine. Add to wok and stir gently until sauce thickens. Mix in remaining 1 tablespoon sesame oil.

Spoon vegetable mixture over soba and serve immediately.

2 SERVINGS

Spicy Tofu and Vegetable Stir-fry with Soba Noodles; Pita Bread with Hummus, Tomatoes and Mint, page 21; Poached Pears with Cranberry-Cardamom Sauce, page 176.

Calzone with Four Cheeses,
Eggplant and Basil

◆ ◆ ◆

7   tablespoons olive oil
4   garlic cloves, minced
¾   pound eggplant, cut into 1-inch cubes

1   tablespoon balsamic vinegar or red wine vinegar

¾   cup pine nuts

1   cup warm water (105°F to 115°F)
1   envelope dry yeast
3   tablespoons olive oil
¾   tablespoon salt
3   cups (or more) bread flour

1½   cups grated Fontina cheese (about 5 ounces)
1½   cups grated mozzarella cheese (about 6 ounces)
1   3.5-ounce log soft mild goat cheese (such as Montrachet),
     crumbled
¼   cup freshly grated Parmesan cheese (about ¾ ounce)

1   red bell pepper, cut into strips
½   cup thinly sliced fresh basil leaves

     Fresh basil sprigs

Combine oil and garlic in small bowl. Let stand 30 minutes. Place
eggplant in colander. Sprinkle with salt and let stand 30 minutes.

Drain eggplant and pat dry. Heat half of garlic-oil mixture in
heavy large skillet over medium heat. Add eggplant and sauté until
tender, about 8 minutes. Increase heat to high. Add vinegar and
cook until almost no liquid remains in skillet, about 1 minute. Season to taste with pepper. Transfer to large bowl.

Heat 1 teaspoon garlic-oil mixture in heavy small skillet over
medium heat. Add pine nuts and sauté until golden, about 2 minutes. Add to eggplant. *(Can be prepared 1 day ahead. Cover and
refrigerate remaining garlic-oil mixture and eggplant mixture separately. Bring to room temperature before using.)*

Place ¼ cup warm water in bowl of heavy-duty mixer; sprinkle yeast over and stir to dissolve. Let stand 10 minutes. Add remaining ¾ cup water, oil, salt and then 3 cups flour; stir to combine.
Attach dough hook to mixer and beat until dough pulls away from
sides of bowl, about 2 minutes. Turn out dough onto lightly floured

surface and knead until smooth and elastic, adding more flour if sticky, about 10 minutes.

Lightly oil large bowl. Add dough, turning to coat. Cover with plastic wrap and let rise in warm draft-free area until doubled in volume, about 1 hour. While dough rises, begin preparation for assembly and baking.

Position rack in lowest third of oven. Place baking stone,* baking tiles* or heavy large rimless baking sheet on rack in oven. Preheat oven to 450°F for 30 minutes. Mix cheeses together in bowl.

Punch dough down. Divide into 4 pieces. Roll out 1 dough piece on lightly floured surface to 8-inch round. Brush dough with some of garlic-oil mixture, leaving 1-inch border. Spread ¼ of cheese mixture over half of dough, leaving 1-inch border. Cover cheese with ¼ of eggplant mixture, ¼ of bell pepper and ¼ of sliced basil leaves. Brush edges of dough with water. Fold dough in half, covering filling but allowing bottom edge of dough to show. Fold bottom edge over top edge and crimp to seal. Repeat with remaining dough, garlic-oil mixture, cheese mixture, eggplant mixture, bell pepper and sliced basil leaves, forming total of 4 calzones. Cover calzones and let stand 15 minutes.

Using large metal spatula, transfer calzones to stone or preheated baking sheet in oven. Bake until golden brown and crisp, about 12 minutes. Transfer calzones to platter. Garnish with basil sprigs and serve.

*Baking stones and tiles are available at cookware stores and many department stores nationwide.

MAKES 4

Gruyère, White Wine and Mustard Fondue

❖ ❖ ❖

5   cups lightly packed grated Gruyère cheese (about 13 ounces)
2 ½ tablespoons all purpose flour
1 ¾ cups dry white wine
2   medium garlic cloves, pressed
¼   cup crumbled Roquefort cheese
¼   cup Dijon mustard
    Steamed red potatoes and bread cubes

Combine Gruyère cheese and flour in large bowl. Simmer wine and garlic in heavy medium saucepan or fondue pot 1 minute. Reduce heat to medium-low. Add Gruyère cheese mixture to saucepan 1 handful at a time, stirring constantly until cheese melts before adding another handful. Whisk in Roquefort cheese (mixture will look grainy). Whisk in mustard. Boil until smooth and thick, stirring constantly, about 2 minutes. Place pot over canned heat burner to keep warm. Serve with potatoes and bread.

4 SERVINGS

Southwest Pinto Bean Skillet Chili

❖ ❖ ❖

2   tablespoons vegetable oil
1   medium onion, chopped
1   green bell pepper, chopped
4   teaspoons chili powder
1   14 ½-ounce can Mexican-style stewed tomatoes
1   14- to 16-ounce can pinto beans or kidney beans, drained
½   cup canned vegetable broth
1 ½ cups shredded hot pepper Monterey Jack cheese

Preheat broiler. In heavy medium skillet with broilerproof handle, heat oil over medium-high heat. Add onion and bell pepper and sauté until vegetables begin to soften, about 6 minutes. Add chili powder and stir 1 minute. Add tomatoes with their juices, beans and broth and simmer until mixture thickens, stirring occasionally, about 10 minutes. Season to taste with salt and pepper. Sprinkle cheese over chili. Broil until cheese melts, about 1 minute.

2 SERVINGS

❖ ❖ ❖

This dish can be served as a main course or an appetizer. Quick and easy to make, it's perfect for spur-of-the-moment entertaining.

❖ ❖ ❖

Vegiburgers in Pita Bread

◆ ◆ ◆

3 cups water
²/₃ cup pearl barley
²/₃ cup brown lentils
²/₃ cup long-grain brown rice

¹/₄ cup vegetable oil
2 cups grated carrots
1 cup chopped onion
1 cup chopped celery
¹/₄ cup shelled sunflower seeds
1 tablespoon minced garlic
1 tablespoon chopped fresh basil or 1 teaspoon dried
2 teaspoons chopped fresh thyme or ¹/₂ teaspoon dried
2 teaspoons chopped fresh oregano or ¹/₂ teaspoon dried

14 pita bread rounds

4 large eggs, beaten to blend
7 tablespoons all purpose flour
   Vegetable oil

   Lettuce leaves
   Sliced tomatoes

Bring 3 cups water to boil in heavy large pot. Stir in barley, lentils and rice. Reduce heat to low. Cover and cook until grains are tender, about 40 minutes. Transfer to large bowl. Drain; cool.

Heat ¹/₄ cup oil in heavy large skillet over medium-low heat. Add carrots, onion, celery, sunflower seeds and garlic and sauté until vegetables are tender, about 12 minutes. Add to grains and cool. Mix in basil, thyme and oregano. Season with salt and pepper. *(Can be made 1 day ahead. Cover and refrigerate.)*

Preheat oven to 300°F. Cut tops off pita rounds to form pockets. Wrap in foil and place in oven to warm.

Stir beaten eggs and flour into grain mixture. Press ¹/₂ cup mixture between palms of hands to form patty. Repeat with remaining mixture. Heat film of oil in heavy large nonstick skillet over medium-high heat. Add patties in batches and cook until golden brown and heated through, about 5 minutes per side.

Place 1 patty in each pita. Top with lettuce and tomatoes.

MAKES ABOUT 14

◆ ◆ ◆

BRIDGE DINNER
FOR EIGHT

ANTIPASTO PLATTER

THREE-GREEN PASTA WITH
SCALLOPS AND PESTO SAUCE,
PAGE 111

ITALIAN BREAD

CHAMPAGNE OR SPARKLING CIDER

VANILLA CREAM AND
APRICOT TART, PAGE 163

◆ ◆ ◆

Orecchiette Pasta with
Peas and Onions

◆ ◆ ◆

2 tablespoons olive oil

2 medium onions, thinly sliced

1½ pounds fresh peas, shelled or 16 ounces frozen, thawed

1 pound orecchiette (little ear-shaped pasta) or other small
   shell pasta

1 cup grated pecorino or Parmesan cheese (about 4 ounces)

Heat olive oil in heavy large skillet over medium heat. Add thinly sliced onions and sauté until golden, about 15 minutes. Add peas and sauté until tender, about 3 minutes.

Meanwhile, add pasta to large pot of boiling salted water and cook until just tender but still firm to bite, stirring often, about 12 minutes. Drain pasta and return to pot. Add onion mixture and ¾ cup grated cheese. Toss to combine. Season to taste with salt and pepper. Transfer pasta to bowl. Sprinkle with remaining ¼ cup cheese and serve immediately.

4 SERVINGS

Fettuccine with
Bacon and Red Peppers

◆ ◆ ◆

2 tablespoons olive oil

1 small onion, sliced

2 bacon slices, chopped

3 garlic cloves, minced

1 7-ounce jar roasted red bell peppers, drained, sliced

1 cup frozen peas, thawed

¼ cup canned chicken broth

12 ounces fettuccine, freshly cooked
   Freshly grated Parmesan

Heat oil in heavy large skillet over medium-high heat. Add onion, bacon and garlic and cook until onion is tender and bacon is cooked, stirring occasionally, about 8 minutes. Stir in peppers, peas and broth and simmer 1 minute. Transfer mixture to large bowl. Add pasta and toss well. Season to taste with salt and pepper. Serve, passing grated Parmesan separately.

4 SERVINGS

Three-Green Pasta
with Scallops and Pesto Sauce

◆ ◆ ◆

1   pound asparagus, trimmed, cut into 1½-inch pieces
½   pound small green beans (preferably haricots verts),
     trimmed, cut into 1½-inch pieces
1   pound fettuccine

3   tablespoons butter
1   10-ounce package frozen peas, thawed
2   pounds sea scallops, each quartered

1½ cups purchased pesto sauce
¾   cup whipping cream
2   tablespoons fresh lemon juice

Bring large pot of salted water to boil. Add asparagus and green beans and cook until just crisp-tender, about 5 minutes. Transfer vegetables to bowl, using strainer. Add fettuccine to water and boil until just tender but still firm to bite, stirring pasta occasionally.

Meanwhile, melt 1½ tablespoons butter in heavy large skillet over medium-high heat. Add asparagus, green beans and peas. Season with salt and pepper; stir until heated through and coated with butter, about 1 minute. Return vegetables to bowl. Melt remaining 1½ tablespoons butter in same skillet. Add quartered sea scallops, season with salt and pepper and sauté until just cooked through, about 1 minute. Remove from heat.

Drain pasta and return to skillet. Add vegetables, scallops, pesto, cream and lemon juice and stir over low heat until pasta is coated with sauce. Season to taste with salt and pepper and serve.

8 SERVINGS

◆ ◆ ◆

Asparagus, green beans and peas give this pasta its name. Start with an antipasto platter of purchased marinated vegetables, cured meats and cheeses. Serve the pasta with some crusty Italian bread. Champagne or sparkling cider makes a festive beverage.

◆ ◆ ◆

Artichoke and Fennel Ravioli with Tomato-Fennel Sauce

❖ ❖ ❖

1   tablespoon olive oil
5   large garlic cloves, chopped
$^{1}/_{4}$ teaspoon fennel seeds
1   9-ounce package frozen artichoke hearts, unthawed
$^{1}/_{2}$ cup chopped fresh fennel
$^{1}/_{2}$ cup canned vegetable broth or water
2   tablespoons minced fresh fennel fronds
1   egg yolk

32   to 36 gyoza (round) wrappers or wonton wrappers
1   egg white

$^{1}/_{4}$ cup olive oil
4   garlic cloves, chopped
1   cup chopped fresh fennel
$1^{1}/_{4}$ teaspoons fennel seeds
1   28-ounce can Italian tomatoes
2   tablespoons tomato paste
1   teaspoon dried oregano, crumbled
$^{1}/_{4}$ teaspoon dried crushed red pepper
$^{1}/_{8}$ teaspoon ground cloves

Fresh fennel fronds

These ravioli are elegant and easy. Frozen artichoke hearts are used for the filling, and purchased *gyoza* wrappers replace homemade pasta.

FOR FILLING: Heat 1 tablespoon olive oil in heavy medium skillet over medium heat. Add 5 chopped garlic cloves and $^{1}/_{4}$ teaspoon fennel seeds and sauté 3 minutes. Add artichoke hearts and $^{1}/_{2}$ cup chopped fennel and stir 1 minute. Add vegetable broth and bring mixture to boil. Cover skillet and cook until vegetables are very tender, about 12 minutes. Uncover and simmer until pan juices have evaporated completely, stirring occasionally, about 10 minutes. Scrape filling into processor and cool. Add 2 tablespoons fennel fronds and process to coarse puree. Season with salt and pepper. Add yolk and blend.

Line baking sheet with plastic wrap. If using wonton wrappers, trim edges to form rounds. Brush entire surface of 1 wrapper lightly with egg white. Place 1 rounded teaspoon filling in center. Fold dough over, forming semi-circle. Seal edges, pressing out any air around filling. Place on prepared sheet. Repeat with remaining filling and wrappers. *(Ravioli can be prepared ahead. Cover loosely with towel and plastic wrap and refrigerate up to 8 hours, or cover with plastic and freeze 3 days. Do not thaw before cooking.)*

FOR SAUCE: Heat ¼ cup oil in heavy large saucepan over medium-low heat. Add 4 garlic cloves, 1 cup fennel and 1¼ teaspoons fennel seeds and sauté until tender, about 12 minutes. Add tomatoes with their juices and next 4 ingredients. Simmer until sauce thickens, breaking up tomatoes with back of spoon, about 25 minutes. Season with salt and pepper. *(Can be made 2 days ahead. Cover; chill. Rewarm before using.)*

Boil ravioli in large pot of boiling salted water until tender, about 5 minutes. Drain well. Spoon some sauce on each plate. Arrange ravioli atop sauce. Garnish with fresh fennel fronds.

8 SERVINGS

Fusilli with Mint Pesto, Potatoes and Goat Cheese

◆ ◆ ◆

1	large fresh parsley bunch, stems trimmed
15	large fresh mint leaves
10	large fresh basil leaves
1	teaspoon salt
5	tablespoons unsalted butter, room temperature
¼	cup grated Parmesan cheese
1	pound small red potatoes, cut into ½-inch pieces
1	pound fusilli or rotelle pasta
1	cup whipping cream
4	ounces goat cheese, crumbled
	Chopped fresh mint leaves

Finely chop first 4 ingredients in processor. Blend in butter and Parmesan. Cover and chill pesto until ready to use. *(Can be made up to 2 days ahead; keep chilled.)*

Cook potatoes in large saucepan of boiling salted water until tender, about 7 minutes. Drain. Cook pasta in large pot of boiling salted water until just tender but still firm to bite, stirring occasionally. Drain well. Transfer to large bowl.

Meanwhile, boil cream in heavy large skillet until slightly thickened, 5 minutes. Whisk in pesto. Add potatoes and heat through.

Pour potatoes and sauce over pasta and toss to coat. Season with salt and pepper. Sprinkle goat cheese and chopped mint over.

4 SERVINGS

PASTA TIPS

Who doesn't love pasta? It's versatile, delicious and downright nutritious. For perfect results every time you cook pasta, here are some tips.

◆ Cook pasta in plenty of boiling water — five quarts per pound.

◆ Stir pasta occasionally while cooking to prevent sticking.

◆ Add salt to the cooking water, if you like, but don't add oil, since oil coats the pasta and causes it to repel the sauce.

◆ Boil pasta just until it is firm to the bite, or *al dente*; be careful not to overcook it.

◆ Adding a glass of cold water to the pasta as soon as it's done will stop the cooking process.

◆ Do not overdrain pasta; some water clinging to the noodles makes them easier to combine with the sauce.

◆ Don't rinse pasta after draining, an unnecessary step that only serves to cool the pasta you want hot.

◆ ◆ ◆

Linguine with Spicy Clam and Mussel Sauce

◆ ◆ ◆

The clams and mussels in this delicious pasta are cooked without liquid so that their flavorful juices are not diluted. Serve with bread and a green salad, and pour a crisp Italian Red wine, like Dolcetto or Nebbiolo d'Alba.

◆ ◆ ◆

$^1/_4$ cup olive oil

5   large garlic cloves, minced

$^1/_2$ teaspoon dried crushed red pepper

2   28-ounce cans Italian plum tomatoes, chopped with juices

1   tablespoon dried oregano

3   pounds small clams, scrubbed

2   pounds mussels, scrubbed, debearded

$1^1/_4$ pounds linguine

$^1/_2$ cup chopped fresh Italian parsley

Heat oil in heavy large saucepan over medium heat. Add garlic and sauté until tender, about 5 minutes. Add crushed red pepper and stir 30 seconds. Add tomatoes with their juices and oregano. Boil gently until thick, stirring occasionally, about 45 minutes. *(Can be prepared 1 day ahead. Cover and refrigerate.)*

Place clams in large pot. Cover and cook over high heat until clams open, about 10 minutes. Using slotted spoon, transfer clams

to bowl. Discard any clams that do not open. Add mussels to same pot. Cover and cook until mussels open, about 6 minutes. Transfer mussels to bowl with clams, discarding any that do not open. Drain shellfish juices from pot into sauce, discarding any sand at bottom. Return clams and mussels to pot; cover to keep warm.

Meanwhile, cook linguine in large pot of boiling salted water until just tender but still firm to bite.

Add parsley to sauce and bring to boil. Season to taste with salt and pepper. Pour sauce over shellfish. Drain pasta and transfer to large shallow bowl. Pour shellfish with sauce over and gently lift pasta to distribute sauce evenly.

6 SERVINGS

Pig in a Haystack

◆ ◆ ◆

2 tablespoons olive oil
3/4 pound mushrooms, sliced
1 6-ounce package thinly sliced Canadian bacon, cut into matchstick-size strips
1 green onion bunch, chopped
2 tablespoons (generous) drained capers
1/2 pound vermicelli, freshly cooked
1 cup grated Parmesan cheese
1/2 cup whipping cream
1/4 cup pine nuts, toasted
Additional grated Parmesan cheese

Heat oil in heavy large skillet over medium heat. Add mushrooms; sauté until tender and beginning to brown, about 10 minutes. Add bacon, green onions and capers; toss to combine. Add vermicelli, 1 cup Parmesan, cream and pine nuts; toss until sauce thickens and coats pasta and mixture is heated through. Season with salt and pepper. Transfer pasta to large shallow bowl. Serve, passing additional Parmesan separately.

4 SERVINGS

◆ ◆ ◆

The "pig" in this recipe is bacon; the "haystack" is vermicelli pasta. With all the ingredients ready, the dish goes from start to finish in minutes.

◆ ◆ ◆

The western Trapanese coast of Sicily is known for recipes with Arab influences. Ground almonds are typical of classical Arabic cooking and turn up here in an easy pasta sauce. Precede this dish with a refreshing salad of sliced oranges and fennel in a simple vinaigrette.

◆ ◆ ◆

Spaghetti with Pesto Trapanese

◆ ◆ ◆

1   cup slivered almonds
6   garlic cloves
1   cup packed coarsely chopped fresh basil leaves
6   large plum tomatoes, peeled, seeded, coarsely chopped
1/2   cup plus 2 tablespoons olive oil

1   pound spaghetti
    Slivered fresh basil
4   large plum tomatoes, seeded, chopped
    Grated Pecorino Romano cheese

Grind almonds and garlic in processor. Add 1 cup basil and chop finely. Add 6 peeled tomatoes and chop finely. Add oil and puree until almost smooth. Season with salt and pepper. *(Can be prepared 6 hours ahead. Cover and chill.)*

Cook spaghetti in large pot of boiling salted water until tender but still firm to bite. Drain. Return to pot. Add sauce and toss to coat. Transfer to large bowl. Top with slivered basil and tomatoes. Serve, passing cheese separately.

4 SERVINGS

Peppery Pasta with Feta Cheese

◆ ◆ ◆

2   tablespoons olive oil
1   large red bell pepper, diced
1   large green bell pepper, diced
6   large garlic cloves, chopped
1   cup thinly sliced stemmed drained peperoncini (about one 16-ounce jar)
1/2   cup chopped fresh basil or 2 tablespoons dried
1   28-ounce can Italian plum tomatoes with juices
1   pound bow-tie pasta, freshly cooked
8   ounces feta cheese, coarsely crumbled

Heat oil in heavy Dutch oven over medium-high heat. Add both bell peppers and garlic. Sauté until peppers begin to soften, about 4 minutes. Mix in peperoncini and basil, then tomatoes. Simmer until sauce reduces slightly, breaking up tomatoes with back of spoon, about 5 minutes. Add pasta and toss until sauce coats pasta. Add feta and toss mixture to blend.

6 SERVINGS

Fettuccine al Pesto

◆ ◆ ◆

1	tablespoon butter
6	ounces thinly sliced prosciutto, cut into thin strips
3	shallots, minced
1	red bell pepper, chopped
2	large garlic cloves, minced
1/2	cup dry white wine
1	cup whipping cream
1/2	cup pesto sauce
1	pound fettuccine noodles
1/4	cup pine nuts, toasted

Melt butter in heavy large saucepan over medium-low heat. Add prosciutto, shallots, bell pepper and garlic. Sauté until bell pepper is tender, about 5 minutes. Add wine and boil until reduced by half, about 3 minutes. Mix in cream and pesto. Cook until sauce thickens, about 5 minutes. Season with salt and pepper.

Meanwhile, bring pot of salted water to boil. Add noodles and cook until tender. Drain. Place in bowl. Pour sauce over and toss. Top with nuts. Serve immediately.

4 TO 6 SERVINGS

Pasta Shells Filled with
Feta and Herbs

◆ ◆ ◆

Basil and chives accent the luscious ricotta and feta cheese stuffing in this comforting main course. Conclude supper with fruit and your favorite cookies.

◆ ◆ ◆

Pasta Shells Filled with Feta and Herbs; Olive Focaccia with Pancetta and Onion Topping, page 154; Fennel and Walnut Salad, page 149; Fresh Fruit and Cookies.

¹/₄   *cup olive oil*

1   *onion, chopped*

2   *garlic cloves, minced*

¹/₄   *teaspoon dried crushed red pepper*

2   *28-ounce cans Italian plum tomatoes, chopped in processor with juices*

1   *cup chopped fresh basil*

2   *15-ounce containers ricotta cheese*

14   *ounces feta cheese, chopped*

¹/₂   *cup chopped fresh basil*

2   *fresh chive bunches, chopped*

2   *eggs*

1   *12-ounce package jumbo pasta shells*

Fresh basil sprigs

FOR SAUCE: Heat oil in heavy large saucepan over medium heat. Add onion and sauté 5 minutes. Add garlic and sauté until onion is tender, about 5 minutes. Add crushed red pepper and sauté 30 seconds. Add tomatoes. Simmer until sauce is reduced to 5 cups, stirring occasionally, about 1 hour. Season to taste with salt and pepper. Remove from heat and mix in 1 cup basil. *(Can be prepared 1 day ahead. Cover and refrigerate.)*

FOR FILLING: Combine ricotta, 1¹/₃ cups feta, ¹/₂ cup chopped basil and chives. Season to taste with salt and pepper. Mix in eggs.

Cook shells in large pot of boiling salted water until just tender but still firm to bite. Drain. Rinse with cold water until cool. Drain thoroughly.

Preheat oven to 350°F. Spread ³/₄ cup sauce over bottom of each of two 13 x 9 x 2-inch glass baking dishes. Fill 30 shells and divide between dishes. Top with remaining sauce. Sprinkle with remaining feta. *(Can be prepared 1 day ahead. Cover and refrigerate.)* Bake shells until heated through, about 30 minutes. Garnish with basil sprigs. Serve immediately.

6 SERVINGS

Pizza with Pesto and
Smoked Salmon

◆ ◆ ◆

1   All Ready Pie Crust (half of 15-ounce package)
½   cup ricotta cheese
3   tablespoons purchased pesto sauce
3   tablespoons pine nuts
3   ounces thinly sliced smoked salmon, cut into 1-inch pieces
    Fresh basil sprig

Preheat oven to 400°F. Lay pie crust in center of baking sheet.
Fold in ½ inch of crust edge. Stand up double edge and crimp decoratively, forming upright rim. Blend cheese and pesto in small bowl.
Spread cheese mixture over crust. Sprinkle with pine nuts. Bake
pizza until crust is set and golden, about 18 minutes.

Arrange salmon pieces over pizza. Garnish with basil and serve.

4 SERVINGS

Superfast Vegetarian Pizza

◆ ◆ ◆

1   tablespoon olive oil
1   medium zucchini, diced
1   medium-size yellow crookneck squash, diced
½   teaspoon dried crushed red pepper

1   16-ounce baked cheese pizza crust (such as Boboli)
1   14-ounce jar mushroom pizza sauce
3   large garlic cloves, minced
1   cup packed shredded mozzarella cheese (about 4 ounces)
½   cup drained oil-packed sun-dried tomatoes, thinly sliced
⅓   cup grated Parmesan cheese

Preheat oven to 450°F. Heat oil in heavy medium skillet over
medium heat. Add zucchini, yellow squash and crushed red pepper; sauté until vegetables are almost tender, about 5 minutes.

Place pizza crust on baking sheet. Spread mushroom sauce
over. Sprinkle with garlic, then mozzarella. Top with squash mixture
and tomatoes. Sprinkle with Parmesan cheese. Bake pizza until
cheese melts and crust is crisp, about 13 minutes. Cut into 8 pieces.

MAKES 8 PIECES

Pronto Pizzas Deluxe

◆ ◆ ◆

2   tablespoons olive oil

4   small leeks (white part only), sliced crosswise

2   large red bell peppers, thinly sliced, halved crosswise

¼   teaspoon dried crushed red pepper

⅔   pound turkey Italian sausage (about 6 small), casings removed

2   16-ounce baked cheese pizza crusts (such as Boboli)

½   cup olive paste (olivada)*

1½   pounds mozzarella cheese, grated

⅔   cup chopped fresh basil

Heat oil in heavy large skillet over medium-high heat. Add leeks and bell peppers and sauté until just tender, about 8 minutes. Add crushed red pepper and stir 30 seconds. Transfer to plate. Add sausage to skillet and cook until no longer pink, crumbling with fork, about 4 minutes. Transfer to another plate. *(Can be prepared 1 day ahead. Cover vegetables and sausage separately and chill.)*

Preheat oven to 450°F. Place pizza crusts on pizza pans or baking sheets. Spread ¼ cup olive paste over each. Top with cheese. Divide sausage and vegetables between pizzas. Bake until cheese melts, about 15 minutes. Top with basil.

*An olive spread available at Italian markets and specialty foods stores. If unavailable, use pureed, pitted, black brine-cured olives (such as Kalamata).

6 SERVINGS

Prepared pizza crusts have revolutionized pizza-making for the home cook. At most supermarkets across the country, you can buy either the rolled out, raw crust (often in a kit, complete with sauce and toppings) or Bobolis, baked cheese pizza crusts. Bobolis are available in the bread section, specialty foods aisle or on a highly trafficked corner of the store. They come wrapped in plastic, often hanging in a display that features different sizes. Just add whatever toppings you like for pizza that bakes up in minutes.

In this recipe, Bobolis are topped with leeks, bell peppers, turkey sausage, mozzarella cheese and basil. Serve with ice cold beer.

◆ ◆ ◆

◆ On the Side ◆

While there will always be those times when the likes of steamed broccoli is the only side dish you have time for, there are other days and meals that call out for a little extra effort in the on-the-side department. That's when this chapter—with its more than 45 recipes for vegetables, grains, salads, sauces and breads—will come in handy.

Whether you're looking for something new to serve with steak or something simple to accompany a more involved main course, a different take on your daily salad or a quick-to-bake bread that promises a fragrant kitchen, the ideal recipe is only a turn of the page away. (To go with that steak, for example, flip over to the Classic French Fries with Chili Salt and Cumin Catsup on page 131.) You may never just steam your broccoli again.

Garden-fresh Herbs, Wild Mushrooms, Red Hot Chilies, Crunchy Biscotti and much more — some of the top food trends of the year.

Sautéed Broccoli Rabe with Garlic

◆ ◆ ◆

1/2 cup olive oil
10 garlic cloves
4 pounds broccoli rabe, trimmed

Divide oil and garlic between 2 heavy large skillets. Cook over medium heat until garlic is golden. Discard garlic. Divide broccoli rabe between skillets and cook until crisp-tender, turning occasionally, about 8 minutes. Season with salt and pepper. Transfer to bowl.

8 SERVINGS

Stir-fried Vegetables with Garlic and Ginger

◆ ◆ ◆

1 teaspoon peanut oil
1/2 teaspoon oriental sesame oil
3 medium carrots (about 14 ounces), cut diagonally into 1/8-inch-thick slices
1/2 pound sugar snap peas or snow peas
1/2 red bell pepper, cut into 1-inch triangles
6 large garlic cloves, thinly sliced
1 tablespoon low-sodium soy sauce
1 teaspoon minced peeled fresh ginger

Heat peanut oil and sesame oil in heavy large nonstick skillet over medium-high heat. Add carrots, cover and cook 2 minutes, stirring once or twice. Add remaining ingredients and stir-fry until vegetables are crisp-tender, about 3 minutes. Divide among plates and serve.

4 SERVINGS

Sesame Asparagus

◆ ◆ ◆

1½ pounds asparagus, trimmed

2 tablespoons (¼ stick) unsalted butter
1 teaspoon oriental sesame oil
4 teaspoons fresh lemon juice
1 teaspoon soy sauce
 Toasted sesame seeds

Cook asparagus in large skillet of boiling salted water until almost crisp-tender, about 5 minutes. Drain asparagus. Transfer to bowl of ice water and cool. Drain and pat dry. *(Can be prepared 1 day ahead. Cover and chill.)*

Melt butter with sesame oil in heavy large skillet over medium-high heat. Add asparagus and sauté until crisp-tender, about 2 minutes. Mix in lemon juice and soy sauce and toss to coat. Season to taste with salt and pepper. Transfer to platter. Sprinkle with sesame seeds and serve.

6 SERVINGS

Sautéed Baby Vegetables

◆ ◆ ◆

3 bunches baby carrots, tops trimmed, peeled
3 bunches baby turnips, tops trimmed, peeled
18 baby zucchini

3 tablespoons unsalted butter

Steam carrots and turnips until crisp-tender, about 5 minutes. Transfer vegetables to bowl of ice water and cool. Steam zucchini until crisp-tender, about 3 minutes. Transfer to ice water and cool. Drain vegetables and pat dry. *(Vegetables can be prepared 6 hours ahead. Cover and refrigerate.)*

Melt butter in heavy large skillet over medium-high heat. Add vegetables and toss just until heated through, about 3 minutes. Season to taste with salt and pepper.

6 SERVINGS

Minted Sugar Snap Peas and Pearl Onions in Brown Butter

◆ ◆ ◆

1   *1-pint basket pearl onions*
2   *pounds sugar snap peas, stringed*

¼   *cup (½ stick) unsalted butter*
¼   *cup chopped fresh mint leaves*

Cook onions in saucepan of boiling water until crisp-tender, about 7 minutes. Using slotted spoon, transfer to bowl of ice water. Return water in saucepan to boil. Add peas; cook until crisp-tender, about 3 minutes. Drain. Transfer to bowl of ice water and cool. Drain onions and peas. Peel onions. *(Can be made 1 day ahead. Cover vegetables; chill.)*

Cook butter in heavy large skillet over medium-high heat until butter browns, about 2 minutes. Add onions, peas and mint and sauté until heated through, about 1 minute. Season with salt and pepper.

12 SERVINGS

Spinach with Olives, Raisins and Pine Nuts

◆ ◆ ◆

3   *10-ounce packages ready-to-use fresh spinach leaves or 4 large bunches, trimmed*

¼   *cup olive oil*
4   *large garlic cloves, chopped*
⅓   *cup (generous) pitted quartered brine-cured olives (such as Kalamata)*
⅓   *cup (generous) raisins*
¼   *cup pine nuts, toasted*
1½   *tablespoons balsamic vinegar or red wine vinegar*

Place colander over large bowl. Line colander with kitchen towel. Toss ⅓ of spinach in heavy Dutch oven over high heat until wilted but still bright green, about 3 minutes. Transfer spinach to prepared colander. Repeat with remaining spinach in 2 batches. Let spinach cool briefly. Gather towel around spinach and squeeze well, pressing out as much liquid as possible. *(Can be prepared 8 hours ahead. Cover and refrigerate.)*

A classic Italian side dish. Use the convenient packaged spinach if it's available in your market.

◆ ◆ ◆

Heat olive oil in heavy large skillet over medium heat. Add chopped garlic, olives and raisins and sauté until garlic begins to color, about 3 minutes. Add spinach and toasted pine nuts and toss until heated through. Add vinegar and toss. Season spinach generously with salt and pepper and serve.

8 SERVINGS

Fennel and Leek Flans

◆ ◆ ◆

1   pound fennel bulbs, trimmed, fronds reserved
2   tablespoons (¼ stick) unsalted butter
2   tablespoons olive oil
⅔   cup chopped leeks (white part only)
1   cup water

1   cup half and half
½   cup freshly grated Parmesan cheese (about 1½ ounces)
2   large eggs, beaten to blend
2   egg yolks
1   teaspoon fennel seeds, crushed in mortar with pestle
½   teaspoon grated nutmeg
½   teaspoon salt

Preheat oven to 350°F. Oil six ½-cup soufflé cups. Line bottoms with waxed-paper rounds. Brush with oil. Set cups on baking sheet. Cut fennel crosswise in half. Slice enough fennel into thin strips to measure 2½ cups. Melt butter with oil in heavy large skillet over medium-high heat. Add fennel and leeks and sauté 5 minutes. Add 1 cup water, cover, reduce heat to low and cook until vegetables are tender, about 15 minutes.

Drain vegetables through sieve, pressing with back of spoon to remove as much liquid as possible. Puree vegetables in processor. Add half and half, cheese, eggs, yolks, fennel seeds, nutmeg and salt. Puree just until blended. *(Can be prepared 1 day ahead. Cover fennel mixture and refrigerate.)*

Divide fennel mixture among prepared cups. Bake flans until puffed and knife inserted into centers comes out clean, about 25 minutes. Cool 5 minutes. Run small sharp knife around sides of flans to loosen. Turn out flans onto plates. Garnish with reserved fennel fronds and serve.

MAKES 6

A sophisticated side dish. The creamy custard can be made a day ahead and baked just before serving.

◆ ◆ ◆

When people work together on a dinner, it takes a lot of pressure off the host — and it's a lot of fun, too. Here are some tips on coordinating a party where everyone helps out.

◆ Select a theme for the menu, then assign a course to each guest. Ask the guests to let you know what they plan to prepare so that you can keep an eye out for overlapping ingredients or similar types of dishes.

◆ Have your guests bring any special equipment they might need for their particular dish.

◆ Either ask each guest to bring a wine or other beverage that goes well with their dish or plan the wine selection yourself, since you'll be familiar with the entire menu.

◆ Start this party on the early side so that each guest will have enough time to finish up whatever needs doing in the kitchen.

◆ ◆ ◆

Green Bean Bundles

◆ ◆ ◆

1   large carrot, peeled
1¹/₂ pounds green beans, trimmed

3   tablespoons unsalted butter
2   garlic cloves, minced
    Red bell pepper strips (optional)
    Lemon peel strips (optional)

Using vegetable peeler, scrape 8 long strips from carrot. Bring large pot of water to boil. Add carrot strips and cook until limp, about 45 seconds. Transfer carrot to work surface; cool. Add beans to same pot and boil until crisp-tender, about 5 minutes. Drain. Refresh under cold water and drain again.

Using heavy large knife, trim sides of each carrot strip to even. Gather 8 to 12 green beans in bundle. Wrap 1 carrot strip around bundle and tie in knot. Trim carrot ends if necessary. Repeat with remaining beans and carrot strips. *(Can be made 8 hours ahead. Cover and refrigerate.)*

Place green bean bundles in steamer and heat through. Melt butter in heavy small skillet over medium heat. Add garlic; sauté 30 seconds. Place bundles on platter. Brush with butter. Season with salt and pepper. Garnish with bell pepper and lemon.

8 SERVINGS

Caramelized Onion and Garlic Tart

◆ ◆ ◆

1¹/₄ cups unbleached all purpose flour
¹/₂   teaspoon salt
5   tablespoons chilled unsalted butter, cut into pieces
2   tablespoons chilled solid vegetable shortening
3   tablespoons (about) ice water

2   tablespoons olive oil
2¹/₂ pounds onions, chopped
10   large garlic cloves, chopped
1   large fresh thyme sprig or ¹/₄ teaspoon dried
1   bay leaf
¹/₂   cup dry white wine

1   cup packed shredded Gruyère cheese (about 4 ounces)

FOR CRUST: Combine flour and salt in processor. Add butter and shortening and cut in using on/off turns until mixture resembles coarse meal. Blend in enough water by tablespoons until dough forms moist clumps. Gather dough into ball; flatten into disk. Wrap in plastic. Refrigerate 30 minutes. *(Dough can be prepared 4 days ahead. Let soften slightly before continuing.)*

Preheat oven to 400°F. Roll out dough on lightly floured surface to 12-inch round. Roll up dough on rolling pin; transfer to 9-inch-diameter tart pan with removable bottom. Press dough into pan; trim edges. Freeze crust 15 minutes.

Line crust with foil. Fill with pie weights or dried beans. Bake crust until set, about 15 minutes. Remove foil and weights. Continue baking until crust is golden brown, piercing with fork if crust bubbles, about 15 minutes longer. Transfer to rack; cool completely.

FOR FILLING: Heat oil in heavy large skillet over medium heat. Add onions, garlic, thyme and bay leaf and cook until onions brown and mixture is jam-like, stirring occasionally, about 50 minutes. Add wine; stir until almost all liquid evaporates, about 5 minutes. Season with salt and pepper. Cool. *(Crust and filling can be made 6 hours ahead. Cover separately; let stand at room temperature.)*

Preheat oven to 400°F. Remove thyme sprig and bay leaf from filling. Stir in Gruyère. Transfer filling to crust. Bake until filling is brown, about 20 minutes. Remove pan sides from tart. Serve tart warm or at room temperature.

8 SERVINGS

Chili Potatoes

◆ ◆ ◆

4   russet potatoes, *thinly sliced*
3   tablespoons olive oil
2   teaspoons chili powder

Preheat oven to 450°F. Place potatoes in bowl. Add 3 tablespoons olive oil and 2 teaspoons chili powder. Season with salt and pepper and mix to coat. Place potatoes in single layer on 2 baking sheets. Bake until beginning to crisp, about 12 minutes per side. Serve hot.

4 SERVINGS

◆ ◆ ◆

Oven-baked potato "chips" at their best—and easiest.

◆ ◆ ◆

Mashed Potatoes and Butternut Squash

♦ ♦ ♦

2 ½ pounds russet potatoes, peeled, cubed
2 ½ pounds butternut squash, peeled, seeded, cubed
8   large garlic cloves
¼   pound (1 stick) margarine, room temperature
     Ground nutmeg

Bring 1 inch of water to boil in large pot. Set steamer rack in pot. Place potatoes, squash and garlic on rack. Cover pot and steam vegetables until tender, adding more water to pot if necessary, about 15 minutes. Transfer vegetables to large bowl. Add margarine and mash vegetables until fairly smooth. Season to taste with nutmeg, salt and pepper. *(Can be prepared 2 hours ahead. Let stand at room temperature. Reheat uncovered in 350°F oven for 30 minutes.)*

8 SERVINGS

Potato-Turnip Gratin with Horseradish Cream

♦ ♦ ♦

1 ¼ cups whipping cream
1 ¼ cups half and half
2   pounds russet potatoes, peeled, thinly sliced
1 ¼ pounds turnips, peeled, halved, thinly sliced
¼   cup cream-style horseradish
1   teaspoon minced fresh rosemary or ½ teaspoon dried

Preheat oven to 400°F. Lightly butter 8 x 8 x 2-inch glass baking dish. Bring cream and half and half to boil in heavy large Dutch oven over medium-high heat. Add potatoes and turnips. Simmer until vegetables just begin to soften, stirring occasionally, about 5 minutes. Using slotted spoon, transfer vegetables to prepared dish. Mix horseradish and rosemary into liquids in pot. Season generously with salt and pepper. Pour liquids over vegetables. Press vegetables firmly to compact. Cover dish with foil. Bake 40 minutes. Uncover and bake gratin until vegetables are tender and top is brown, about 30 minutes longer. Let stand 10 minutes.

6 TO 8 SERVINGS

Classic French Fries with Chili Salt and Cumin Catsup

$\blacklozenge$ $\blacklozenge$ $\blacklozenge$

$^1/_2$ cup catsup

1 teaspoon ground cumin

1 teaspoon balsamic vinegar or red wine vinegar

2 teaspoons salt

2 teaspoons chili powder

3 large russet potatoes, peeled, wiped dry, cut into generous $^1/_4$-inch-thick sticks
    Canola oil (for deep frying)

Combine catsup, cumin and vinegar in small bowl. Combine salt and chili powder in another small bowl. *(Can be prepared 1 day ahead. Cover separately and let stand at room temperature.)*

Arrange potatoes in parallel rows on kitchen towel. Roll towel up, enclosing potatoes, and let stand at least 30 minutes and up to 1 hour to dry potatoes.

Pour oil into heavy large saucepan to depth of 3 inches. Attach deep-fry thermometer and heat oil over medium-high heat to 320°F. Add $^1/_4$ of potatoes to oil and fry until just tender and barely colored, about 3 minutes. Using slotted spoon, transfer potatoes to wire rack set over paper towels and allow to drain. Reheat oil to 320°F if necessary. Repeat frying with remaining potatoes in 3 more batches. Cool completely. *(Can be prepared up to 3 hours ahead. Let potatoes stand at room temperature; let oil cool.)*

Reheat oil to 400°F. Fry potatoes in 3 batches until deep golden brown and beginning to blister, about 2 minutes. Using slotted spoon, transfer potatoes to basket lined with several layers of paper towels. Sprinkle with chili salt and serve with cumin catsup.

2 GENEROUS SERVINGS

Tarragon-Butter Sautéed Potatoes

◆ ◆ ◆

2 pounds white-skinned potatoes

3 tablespoons Tarragon Butter (see recipe below)
4 shallots, sliced
   Minced fresh tarragon

In large pot of boiling water, cook potatoes until tender. Drain and cool. Peel potatoes. Cut into ³/₄-inch pieces.

Melt butter in heavy large skillet over medium-high heat. Add shallots and sauté 1 minute. Add potatoes. Season with salt and pepper and stir until heated through. Sprinkle with tarragon.

4 SERVINGS

Tarragon Butter

³/₄ cup (1¹/₂ sticks) butter, room temperature
3   tablespoons minced fresh tarragon or 1 tablespoon dried
2   large shallots, minced
1   tablespoon Dijon mustard

Combine all ingredients. Mix in generous amount of pepper. (Can be made 2 days ahead. Cover and chill.)

MAKES ABOUT 1 CUP

Sweet-Potato Casserole

◆ ◆ ◆

3   pounds sweet potatoes, peeled, cubed
¹/₄ cup fresh orange juice
¹/₄ cup firmly packed brown sugar
¹/₄ cup (¹/₂ stick) unsalted butter
4   teaspoons grated orange peel
¹/₂ teaspoon ground cinnamon
¹/₄ teaspoon ground nutmeg
    Pinch of ground ginger
2   large eggs, beaten to blend

    Chopped fresh parsley

Cook sweet potatoes in large pot of boiling salted water until tender, about 30 minutes. Drain. Transfer to large bowl. Add juice, sugar, butter, orange peel and spices and mash together. Season with salt and pepper. Mix in eggs. Transfer to 6-cup shallow baking dish. *(Can be prepared 8 hours ahead. Cover and chill.)*

Preheat oven to 350°F. Bake sweet potatoes until heated through and just set, about 45 minutes. Top with parsley.

12 SERVINGS

Gratin Dauphinois

◆ ◆ ◆

1   *garlic clove, halved*
2   *cups whipping cream*
2   *cups milk*
1   *teaspoon ground nutmeg*
3 ½ *pounds russet potatoes, peeled, thinly sliced*
1   *cup grated cheddar cheese*

Preheat oven to 375°F. Rub garlic over inside of 13 x 9-inch baking dish. Place garlic in saucepan. Add cream, milk and nutmeg to saucepan; bring to simmer. Arrange potato slices in 1 layer in dish. Season with salt and pepper. Repeat layering with remaining potatoes, seasoning each layer with salt and pepper. Pour cream mixture over potatoes. Sprinkle with cheese. Bake until potatoes are tender and top is deep golden, about 1 hour 45 minutes. Cool slightly before serving.

8 SERVINGS

Avocado "Pesto"

◆ ◆ ◆

1   *medium avocado, peeled, halved*
1   *cup lightly packed fresh basil leaves*
½   *cup (or more) canned chicken broth*
4   *large garlic cloves*
2   *tablespoons fresh lime juice*
½   *cup vegetable oil*

Place avocado, basil, ½ cup broth, garlic and lime juice in blender. Blend until chopped, scraping down sides as needed. With machine running, gradually add oil and blend until smooth. If too thick, gradually add more broth by tablespoons. Season with salt and pepper.

MAKES ABOUT 2 CUPS

An easy-to-make sauce to accompany grilled chicken or to toss with pasta. Sprinkle the pasta with some crumbled feta cheese before serving.

◆ ◆ ◆

Cranberry-Tangerine Relish with Walnuts

◆ ◆ ◆

2   *large tangerines or 2 small oranges*

3   *cups cranberries*

²/₃   *cup sugar*

¹/₂   *cup chopped toasted walnuts*

Cut 1 tangerine with peel into 6 wedges. Discard seeds. Add to processor; coarsely chop using on/off turns. Add cranberries; coarsely chop using on/off turns. Transfer to large bowl. Peel remaining tangerine and chop coarsely, discarding seeds. Add to cranberry mixture. Add sugar and toss well. *(Can be made 1 day ahead. Cover; chill.)* Mix nuts into relish.

MAKES ABOUT 3 CUPS

Sausage and Herb Stuffing

◆ ◆ ◆

1   *pound egg bread, crusts trimmed, cut into ³/₄-inch cubes*

1   *pound bulk sausage*

¹/₄   *cup (¹/₂ stick) unsalted butter*

3   *large celery stalks, chopped*

1   *large onion, chopped*

1   *large red bell pepper, chopped*

2   *teaspoons poultry seasoning*

1   *teaspoon minced fresh thyme or ¹/₄ teaspoon dried*

1   *teaspoon chopped fresh sage or ¹/₄ teaspoon dried*

³/₄   *cup chicken stock or canned low-salt broth*

2   *eggs, beaten to blend*

¹/₂   *cup chopped fresh parsley*

Preheat oven to 400°F. Arrange bread on baking sheet. Bake until light golden, about 12 minutes. Cool.

Cook sausage in heavy large skillet over medium-high heat until cooked through, crumbling with fork, about 8 minutes. Using slotted spoon, transfer sausage to large bowl. Add butter to any drippings in same skillet; melt over medium-high heat. Add celery, onion, bell pepper, poultry seasoning, thyme and sage to skillet; sauté 10 minutes. Add mixture to sausage, then mix in bread. Add ¾ cup stock to same skillet; bring to boil, scraping up any browned bits. Pour over stuffing. Season with salt and pepper. Add eggs and parsley; toss well.

12 SERVINGS

Curry-spiced Citrus and Avocado Salsa

◆ ◆ ◆

2 large oranges
1 large red grapefruit
1 tablespoon curry powder

1 avocado, peeled, seeded, diced
½ cup chopped red onion
2 tablespoons chopped fresh chives or green onions
1 tablespoon avocado oil or vegetable oil
   Ground white pepper

Cut peel and white pith off oranges and grapefruit. Using small knife and working over heavy small saucepan to catch juice, cut between membranes of fruit to release segments. Using slotted spoon, transfer segments to work surface and chop. Transfer segments to bowl. Scrape juice from work surface into saucepan. Squeeze any remaining juice from citrus membranes into saucepan. Whisk curry powder into juice. Boil until reduced to ¼ cup, about 10 minutes. Cool reduced juice.

Add avocado, onion and chives to citrus segments. Drizzle with oil and 2 tablespoons plus 1 teaspoon reduced juice (reserve remaining juice for another use). Season with salt and white pepper. Toss gently; serve immediately.

MAKES ABOUT 2½ CUPS

◆ ◆ ◆

A lovely array of textures and flavors. Very nice with skewers of grilled scallops or panfried salmon fillets.

Tucson Black and White Bean Salsa

◆ ◆ ◆

3   tablespoons corn oil

1¼ cups fresh corn kernels or frozen, thawed

1   16-ounce can black beans, rinsed, drained

1   15-ounce can Great Northern white beans, drained

1   cup chopped red bell pepper

¾   cup chopped red onion

2   tablespoons fresh lime juice

3   large garlic cloves, pressed

1   large jalapeño chili, seeded, minced

1   tablespoon minced fresh oregano or 1 teaspoon dried

1   tablespoon chili powder

1½ teaspoons ground cumin

Heat 1 tablespoon oil in heavy large skillet over high heat. Add corn and sauté until brown, about 3 minutes. Transfer to large bowl. Add 2 tablespoons oil and all remaining ingredients. Season generously with salt and pepper. *(Can be made 2 days ahead. Cover and chill. Bring to room temperature before serving.)*

MAKES ABOUT 6 CUPS

This is great with tortilla chips as a dip. Or try it as a meatless filling for burritos, adding grated Monterey Jack cheese.

◆ ◆ ◆

Sun-dried Tomato Catsup

◆ ◆ ◆

3   tablespoons chopped dried (not oil-packed) sun-dried tomatoes

1   14½- to 16-ounce can tomatoes with juices

1   tablespoon vegetable oil

½   cup finely chopped onion

1   garlic clove minced

1   tablespoon dark brown sugar

1   tablespoon (or more) cider vinegar

     Dash of hot pepper sauce (such as Tabasco)

Soak sun-dried tomatoes in hot water to cover for 30 minutes. Drain. Purée canned tomatoes with their juices in blender or food processor. Heat vegetable oil in heavy large skillet over medium-low heat. Add onion and garlic and sauté until golden brown and tender, about 10 minutes. Add pureed tomatoes, sun-dried tomatoes, sugar and 1 tablespoon vinegar and bring to boil. Reduce heat to low; simmer until catsup is thick, stirring frequently, about 15 minutes. Add hot pepper sauce and more vinegar if desired. Season with salt.

MAKES ABOUT 1 CUP

Curry Vinaigrette

◆ ◆ ◆

$1/4$ cup dry white wine
1 tablespoon plus $1^1/2$ teaspoons curry powder
$1/2$ teaspoon ground cardamom
$1/2$ cup chopped apple
$3^1/2$ tablespoons chopped peeled fresh ginger
2 tablespoons fresh lime juice
1 hard-boiled egg yolk
$1^1/2$ teaspoons honey
  Pinch of cayenne pepper
$1/2$ cup olive oil
$1/2$ cup corn oil
2 tablespoons chopped cilantro

Bring first 3 ingredients to boil in heavy small saucepan. Transfer to processor. Add apple and next 5 ingredients. Blend until finely chopped. With machine running, gradually add oils. Strain vinaigrette. *(Can be made 1 day ahead. Cover and chill.)* Mix in cilantro before using.

MAKES ABOUT $1^2/3$ CUPS

AN INDOOR PICNIC

CRUDITÉS OF RADISHES AND
BABY CARROTS

ASSORTED CHARCUTERIE
(PATÉS, TERRINES AND SALAMI)

ASSORTED FRENCH CHEESES

FRENCH BREAD BAGUETTES AND
HERB BREADS

PARSLEY BUTTER

MARINATED PROVENÇALE SALAD,
PAGE 141

MUSTARD CHICKEN WITH MIXED
GREENS, PAGE 68

CARAMELIZED ONION AND GARLIC
TART, PAGE 128

RED AND WHITE BURGUNDIES

ALMOND BUTTER COOKIES

FRUIT COMPOTE WITH
CREME FRAICHE

THE CHEESE COURSE

With bistro cooking so big these days, you might want to stage a dinner party with a bistro theme. If you do, don't forget the cheese course, served before dessert and consisting of different cheeses, fresh fruit, nuts and crackers. Here are some cheeses to choose from.

◆ Bleu de Bresse: A mild and creamy blue-veined cheese that goes well with sliced pears and walnuts.

◆ Camembert: This soft and creamy cheese is a lot like Brie, but often milder in flavor.

◆ Cantal: Often called the cheddar of France, Cantal becomes sharper and more crumbly with age.

◆ Chèvre: Made from goat's milk, chèvre has a fresh, tart flavor.

◆ Comté: This is a semihard cheese similar to Gruyère.

◆ St.-André: A "triple-cream" cheese that is soft and buttery.

◆ ◆ ◆

◆ SALADS ◆

Artichoke, Endive and Radicchio Salad with Walnuts

◆ ◆ ◆

4   cups water
1   cup dry white wine
½   onion, sliced
10   whole black peppercorns
1   teaspoon dried thyme, crumbled
2   tablespoons plus 1 teaspoon Sherry wine vinegar or red wine vinegar
2   large artichokes, cut lengthwise in half

1   tablespoon minced shallot
1   tablespoon walnut oil or extra-virgin olive oil

6   cups torn mixed greens (such as curly endive and radicchio)
2   large Belgian endive heads, sliced (about 8 ounces)
2   tablespoons finely chopped toasted walnuts

Combine first 5 ingredients and 2 tablespoons vinegar in heavy large pot. Bring to boil. Add artichokes cut side down. Reduce heat, cover and simmer until artichokes are tender, turning once, about 40 minutes.

Transfer artichokes to bowl using slotted spoon. Discard onion. Boil cooking liquid until reduced to ½ cup, about 20 minutes. Strain liquid into small bowl. Whisk minced shallot, walnut oil and remaining 1 teaspoon vinegar into cooking liquid. Season to taste with salt and pepper. Refrigerate vinaigrette until cold. Remove all artichoke leaves. Scoop out choke and discard. Thinly slice artichoke hearts. *(Can be made 8 hours ahead. Cover and refrigerate vinaigrette and artichoke leaves and hearts separately.)*

Arrange artichoke leaves in spoke pattern around edge of plates. Toss greens and Belgian endive in large bowl with vinaigrette. Divide salad among plates. Tuck artichoke heart slices under greens. Sprinkle with walnuts and serve.

4 SERVINGS

Marinated Provençale Salad

❖ ❖ ❖

4   large red bell peppers, quartered lengthwise
4   yellow zucchini or crookneck squash, thinly sliced lengthwise
    Olive oil
4   medium zucchini, thinly sliced lengthwise
4   large Japanese eggplants, thinly sliced lengthwise

¼   cup minced fresh basil or 1 tablespoon dried
¼   cup minced mixed fresh herbs (such as oregano, marjoram,
    thyme and parsley) or 1 tablespoon dried mixed herbs
3   garlic cloves, pressed
2½ tablespoons olive oil
2½ teaspoons balsamic vinegar or red wine vinegar

6   tomatoes, thinly sliced
¼   cup Niçoise olives*

Preheat broiler. Arrange peppers skin side up on large baking
sheet. Broil until skin blackens. Transfer peppers to plastic bag; set
aside to cool. Arrange yellow zucchini in single layer on same baking sheet. Brush both sides of yellow zucchini with oil. Broil until
almost tender and golden, about 4 minutes per side. Repeat with
zucchini and eggplant slices, brushing with oil before broiling (keep
vegetables separate).

Peel peppers and slice thinly. Mix all herbs and garlic in bowl.
Arrange yellow zucchini on platter. Season with salt and pepper.
Drizzle with 1½ teaspoons oil and ½ teaspoon vinegar. Sprinkle
with ⅕ of herb mixture. Repeat layering with eggplant, peppers
and zucchini, using 1½ teaspoons oil, ½ teaspoon vinegar and ⅕ of
herb mixture for each layer. Cover vegetables and remaining herb
mixture separately; chill overnight. Let stand 1 hour at room temperature before continuing.

Arrange tomato slices atop vegetables. Season with salt and
pepper. Drizzle with remaining 1½ teaspoons oil and ½ teaspoon
vinegar. Top with remaining herb mixture and olives.

*Small, brine-cured black olives available at specialty foods
stores and in some supermarkets.

8 SERVINGS

A great mixture of tastes and textures. You can grill the bread up to two hours ahead of time.

◆ ◆ ◆

Tomato, Blue Cheese and Grilled Bread Salad

◆ ◆ ◆

1/3 cup plus 3 tablespoons olive oil

5 large garlic cloves, minced

6 large 1-inch-thick slices (about 5 x 3 inches) day-old French or Italian bread, crusts trimmed

3 tablespoons Sherry wine vinegar

2 pounds large tomatoes, cored, cut into 1-inch pieces

1 medium red onion, thinly sliced

6 ounces blue cheese, crumbled, room temperature

Combine 1/3 cup olive oil and 3 garlic cloves in small bowl. Let stand 30 minutes at room temperature or refrigerate overnight.

Prepare barbecue (medium-high heat). Brush bread on both sides with garlic oil. Grill until crisp and golden, turning occasionally, about 5 minutes. Cool; cut into 1-inch cubes.

Combine vinegar, 3 tablespoons oil and 2 minced garlic cloves in large bowl. Season generously with salt and pepper. Add tomatoes and onion and let stand 30 minutes, stirring occasionally.

Add bread to tomatoes; toss. Place in large shallow bowl. Top with cheese. Serve immediately.

8 SERVINGS

Lemon Caesar Salad

◆ ◆ ◆

1/2 cup olive oil

1/2 cup freshly grated Parmesan cheese (about 1 1/2 ounces)

1/4 cup fresh lemon juice

1 tablespoon Dijon mustard

1 1/2 teaspoons Worcestershire sauce

2 anchovies, drained

1 large garlic clove

2 heads romaine lettuce, torn into bite-size pieces
    Croutons
    Additional freshly grated Parmesan cheese

Combine first 7 ingredients in processor and blend well. *(Can be prepared 1 day ahead. Cover and refrigerate. Bring to room temperature before using.)* Place lettuce in large bowl. Add enough dressing to coat. Season with salt and pepper. Sprinkle with croutons and additional cheese.

6 SERVINGS

Potato, Beet and Cucumber Salad

◆ ◆ ◆

3   medium beets, stems removed

1³⁄₄ pounds red potatoes, cut into ³⁄₄-inch cubes
2   tablespoons plus 2 teaspoons white wine vinegar

1   English hothouse cucumber, cut into ³⁄₄-inch cubes
1   tablespoon plus 1 teaspoon Dijon mustard
2   teaspoons sugar
6   tablespoons olive oil
2   tablespoons minced fresh dill
1¹⁄₂ teaspoons caraway seeds, crushed in mortar with pestle

     Boston lettuce leaves
     Fresh dill sprigs

Preheat oven to 375°F. Wrap beets in foil. Bake until tender, about 1 hour 15 minutes. Unwrap and cool slightly. Peel beets and cut into ³⁄₄-inch cubes. Place in small bowl.

Cook potatoes in large pot of boiling water until tender. Drain. Transfer to large bowl. Add 2 tablespoons vinegar; stir gently with rubber spatula. Cool.

Add cucumber to potatoes. Mix 2 teaspoons vinegar, mustard and sugar in small bowl. Gradually whisk in oil. Add minced dill and caraway. Toss beets with just enough dressing to coat. Mix remaining dressing into potatoes. Season mixtures with salt and pepper. *(Can be made 1 day ahead. Cover and chill.)*

Just before serving, gently mix beets into potato salad. Line platter with lettuce; top with salad. Garnish with dill.

4 SERVINGS

◆ ◆ ◆

Unlike the typical potato salad, though, this recipe includes fresh beets, which you simply wrap in foil and bake until tender, and chunks of cucumber. Fresh dill and caraway make for an interesting spice bite.

◆ ◆ ◆

Here, arugula (a pungent green) is cut into thin strips and teamed with green beans and robust *crimini* mushrooms and napped with a creamy dressing. For mushrooms with the best texture, choose those with firm, tightly closed heads.

Green Bean and Mushroom Salad with Arugula Chiffonade

❖ ❖ ❖

1   cup mayonnaise
1   cup plain yogurt
2   tablespoons fresh lemon juice

1¼ pounds green beans, trimmed
10 ounces large crimini or button mushrooms, thickly sliced
1   cup thinly sliced arugula (about 2 bunches)

Combine mayonnaise, yogurt and lemon juice in medium bowl and whisk until smooth. Season with salt. *(Can be prepared 1 day ahead. Cover and chill.)*

Cook beans in large pot of boiling salted water until just tender, about 5 minutes. Drain beans. Refresh under cold water; drain and pat dry. Place beans in large bowl. Add mushrooms and toss to combine. Mound salad on platter. Pour dressing over. Season generously with pepper. Top with arugula.

8 SERVINGS

Slightly Newfangled Macaroni Salad

❖ ❖ ❖

½   pound thick bacon slices

12 ounces elbow macaroni or fusilli

2   cups mayonnaise
½   cup (or more) buttermilk
2   tablespoons fresh lemon juice
2   tablespoons Dijon mustard
1   tablespoon sugar
10 ounces crimini or button mushrooms, sliced
1   10-ounce package frozen peas, thawed, drained

1   bunch fresh spinach, trimmed

Cook bacon in large skillet over medium heat until crisp, turning occasionally. Transfer to paper towels and cool. Coarsely chop.

Cook pasta in large pot of boiling salted water until just tender but still firm to bite, stirring occasionally. Drain. Rinse under cold water and drain well.

Whisk mayonnaise, ½ cup buttermilk, lemon juice, mustard and sugar in large bowl. Add pasta, bacon, mushrooms and peas; toss. Season with salt and pepper. *(Can be made 1 day ahead. Cover with plastic wrap and refrigerate. Toss with more buttermilk if dry. Let stand 1 hour before continuing.)*

Line large shallow bowl with spinach leaves. Fill with salad.

12 SERVINGS

Baked Goat Cheese with Garden Salad

◆ ◆ ◆

½ cup olive oil

4 *fresh thyme sprigs or 1 teaspoon dried*

1 *bay leaf, crumbled*

2 *4-ounce logs soft mild goat cheese (such as Montrachet), each cut into four ½-inch-thick rounds*

1 *cup toasted fresh white breadcrumbs*

3 *tablespoons balsamic vinegar or 2 tablespoons red wine vinegar*

8 *cups assorted baby greens (such as arugula, oakleaf and red leaf)*

Combine first 3 ingredients in small bowl. Arrange cheese rounds in single layer in small glass baking dish. Pour oil mixture over cheese. Turn cheese to coat. Cover and refrigerate 1 day.

Preheat oven to 450°F. Lightly oil baking sheet. Place breadcrumbs in bowl. Remove cheese from oil; reserve oil. Coat each round with crumbs, pressing gently to adhere. Arrange cheese on prepared baking sheet. Bake until golden, about 5 minutes.

Whisk vinegar into reserved oil mixture. Season with salt and pepper. Place greens in bowl. Pour over enough vinaigrette to coat lightly. Season with salt and pepper. Top salad with hot cheese.

4 SERVINGS

◆ ◆ ◆

Begin marinating the goat cheese for this innovative salad one day before you plan to serve it.

Tricolor Salad with Honey-Cumin Dressing

◆ ◆ ◆

6   tablespoons olive oil
3   tablespoons balsamic vinegar or red wine vinegar
1¹/₂ teaspoons honey
³/₄   teaspoon ground cumin
³/₄   teaspoon chili powder

1   head butter lettuce, torn into bite-size pieces
1   large watercress bunch, stems trimmed
1   large head radicchio, torn into bite-size pieces
¹/₂ red onion, thinly sliced
2   oranges, peeled, sliced crosswise into rounds

Whisk first 5 ingredients in small bowl to blend. Season dressing with salt and pepper.

Place remaining ingredients in large bowl. Toss salad with enough dressing to season to taste.

4 SERVINGS

Double-Tomato Salad

◆ ◆ ◆

4   large tomatoes, sliced
¼   cup chopped drained oil-packed sun-dried tomatoes
     (2 tablespoons oil reserved)
1   tablespoon olive oil
1   tablespoon balsamic vinegar or red wine vinegar
½   cup green olives (preferably imported), quartered lengthwise
2   tablespoons drained capers
2   tablespoons chopped fresh marjoram or 1 teaspoon dried

Arrange tomatoes on platter. Combine reserved sun-dried tomato oil and 1 tablespoon olive oil in small bowl. Mix in vinegar. Drizzle over tomatoes. Sprinkle with salt and pepper. Top with sun-dried tomatoes and all remaining ingredients.

4 SERVINGS

Couscous Salad with Cinnamon Vinaigrette

◆ ◆ ◆

⅓   cup canola oil
2   teaspoons ground cinnamon
1   teaspoon ground cumin

2⅓ cups canned chicken broth
1   10-ounce box couscous
¾   cup dried cranberries or currants
3   tablespoons minced shallot
2   tablespoons white wine vinegar
5   green onions, chopped
1   15- to 16-ounce can chick-peas (garbanzo beans), drained
5   tablespoons chopped fresh mint

Bring first 3 ingredients to boil in heavy small saucepan, stirring mixture constantly. Pour into small bowl; cool.

Bring broth to boil in heavy medium saucepan. Mix in couscous and cranberries. Cover; remove from heat. Let stand 5 minutes. Transfer to bowl; fluff with fork. Cool. Whisk shallot and vinegar into oil. Pour over couscous. Mix in onions, beans and mint.

4 SERVINGS

◆ ◆ ◆

In this recipe, dried cranberries replace the raisins that usually go into couscous. Serve this delicious and unusual salad as a main course or as a side dish for lamb or chicken.

◆ ◆ ◆

Chino y Latino Salad

♦ ♦ ♦

2 ¹/₂ tablespoons vegetable oil
1   pound yams, cut into ¹/₂-inch dice
1   plantain, cut into ¹/₂-inch dice
1   cup cooked long-grain white rice
1   cup Black Beans with Tomato and Bell Pepper (see recipe, page 12)
1   cup mung bean sprouts
2   red or green bell peppers, chopped
¹/₂   red onion, finely chopped
¹/₂   fresh cilantro bunch, chopped

5   tablespoons fresh lime juice
3   tablespoons olive oil
1 ¹/₂ teaspoons chili oil*
3   garlic cloves, minced
32 large radicchio leaves (about 5 heads)

Heat vegetable oil in large nonstick skillet over medium heat. Add yams; sauté 10 minutes. Add plantain; sauté until yams and plantain are tender, 5 minutes. Transfer to bowl. Mix in rice, beans, sprouts, bell peppers, onion and cilantro.

Mix lime juice, olive and chili oils and garlic. Toss with salad. Season with salt and pepper. Chill at least 3 hours, tossing occasionally. Place radicchio on platter. Fill with salad.

*Available at Asian markets and in many supermarkets.

16 SERVINGS

This title refers to the combination of Chinese ingredients (bean sprouts, chili oil) and Latin American ones (yams, plantain, beans). Be sure the plantain is very ripe, with a deep yellow skin and black spots.

♦ ♦ ♦

Cucumbers with Miso-Sesame Dressing

♦ ♦ ♦

¹/₄   cup white (shiro) miso*
¹/₄   cup rice vinegar
2   tablespoons water
2   teaspoons black sesame seeds*
1   teaspoon sugar

5   pickling cucumbers, thinly sliced
¹/₄   cup chopped green onions

Combine miso, vinegar, water, sesame seeds and sugar in medium bowl. *(Dressing can be prepared 4 hours ahead. Let stand at room temperature.)*

Mix cucumbers and dressing in bowl. Sprinkle onions over.

*Miso (fermented soybean paste) and black sesame seeds are both available at Asian markets and specialty foods stores.

4 SERVINGS

Fennel and Walnut Salad

◆ ◆ ◆

2   large fennel bulbs, trimmed, sliced
2   tablespoons extra-virgin olive oil
1   large head radicchio, separated into 6 outer leaves
1/3   cup chopped walnuts

Place fennel in medium bowl. Add oil and toss to coat. Season to taste with salt and pepper. Place 1 radicchio leaf on each plate. Fill with fennel. Sprinkle with walnuts and serve.

6 SERVINGS

Spicy Marinated Pepper Slaw

◆ ◆ ◆

3   large red bell peppers, cut into matchstick-size strips
2   jalapeño chilies, minced
2/3   cup olive oil
1/2   cup red wine vinegar
3   tablespoons sugar
12   cups thinly sliced green cabbage (about 2 pounds)

Toss peppers and chilies in large bowl. Bring oil, vinegar and sugar just to boil in heavy small saucepan over medium heat, stirring often. Pour over peppers in bowl and toss to coat. Cool. Add cabbage and toss to coat. Season with salt. *(Can be prepared 1 hour ahead. Cover and chill.)*

12 SERVINGS

◆ ◆ ◆

Miso, an Asian soybean paste, is widely available in this country. It adds tangy flavor to this quick dish.

◆ ◆ ◆

*Clockwise from far right: Cheddar
Cheese Loaf; Maslin Rolls; Potato Baps;
Selkirk Bannock.*

There's nothing like rain to dampen your spirits on a day when you had planned a picnic. But it doesn't have to mean the party gets cancelled — just bring the meal indoors. Here are a few tips for transporting an outdoor meal to an indoor setting.

◆ There's no need to change your table. Pack everything up and lay it out on the floor in a cozy corner of the house. Bring in some flowers and greenery (if it's not pouring!) to create an alfresco mood.

◆ If you were planning to serve a grilled dish, use the broiler instead; in most cases, it's the grill's best substitute. Alternatively (depending on how heavy the rain is), grab an umbrella and go ahead and use the grill if it's covered.

◆ Smile, and make the best of the situation. There will be plenty to talk — and laugh — about when it comes time to eat.

◆ ◆ ◆

Cheddar Cheese Loaf

◆ ◆ ◆

$^1\!/_4$ *cup warm water (105°F to 115°F)*
1   *package dry yeast*
1   *teaspoon sugar*
6   *tablespoons milk, room temperature*
2   *teaspoons dry mustard*
$^1\!/_2$ *teaspoon salt*
$1^1\!/_2$ *cups (about) unbleached all purpose flour, sifted*

2   *tablespoons finely chopped onion*
1   *cup grated extra-sharp cheddar cheese (about 4 ounces)*
1   *teaspoon celery seeds*

1   *egg, beaten to blend (glaze)*

Mix water, yeast and sugar in large bowl, stirring to dissolve yeast. Let stand until foamy, about 10 minutes. Mix in milk, mustard and salt. Gradually mix in enough flour to form soft and slightly sticky dough. Turn out dough onto lightly floured surface and knead until smooth and elastic, about 10 minutes. Lightly oil large bowl. Add dough, turning to coat. Cover bowl with plastic wrap and let dough rise in warm draft-free area until doubled in volume, about 1 hour.

Grease 7½ x 3½ x 2¼-inch loaf pan. Punch down dough. Turn out dough onto lightly floured surface. Pinch off ½-inch piece of dough and roll into ball. Repeat with remaining dough. Arrange half of dough balls in bottom of prepared pan. Sprinkle with 1 tablespoon onion, then ½ cup cheese and ½ teaspoon celery seeds. Cover with remaining dough balls. Sprinkle with remaining onion, cheese and celery seeds. Cover pan with plastic wrap. Let dough rise in warm draft-free area until it just reaches top of pan, 1 hour.

Preheat oven to 375°F. Brush loaf with egg glaze. Bake until top is golden brown and bread sounds hollow when tapped on bottom, about 45 minutes. Cool bread in pan 15 minutes. Turn out bread onto rack and cool completely. *(Can be prepared 1 day ahead. Cover and let stand at room temperature.)*

MAKES 1 LOAF

Potato Baps

◆ ◆ ◆

1   medium russet potato (about 8 ounces), peeled, quartered

2¼ cups (about) unbleached all purpose flour
1   package fast-rising dry yeast
2   teaspoons salt

Cook potato in saucepan of boiling water until tender. Drain; reserve ½ cup cooking liquid. Let liquid cool to 125°F to 130°F.

Mash potato in large bowl. Mix in 2 cups flour, yeast and salt. Add reserved ½ cup warm cooking liquid and stir to combine. Mix in enough remaining flour to form soft dough. Turn out dough onto lightly floured surface and knead until smooth and elastic, about 10 minutes. Lightly oil large bowl. Add dough, turning to coat. Cover and let dough rise in warm draft-free area until doubled in volume, about 1½ hours.

Lightly flour heavy large baking sheet. Punch down dough. Turn out dough onto lightly floured surface. Divide dough into 6 pieces. Roll each piece into smooth ball. Arrange on prepared baking sheet, spacing evenly. Cover with towel and let rise until light and puffy, about 40 minutes.

Preheat oven to 425°F. Using rolling pin, gently flatten each ball of dough into 4-inch round. Sprinkle lightly with flour. Bake until rolls are golden brown and sound hollow when tapped on bottom, about 20 minutes. Transfer rolls to rack and cool completely.

MAKES 6

◆ ◆ ◆

Baps are a traditional Scottish breakfast roll. The mashed potato in this recipe yields a soft, light dough.

◆ ◆ ◆

Flowers are a great way to bring color to the table and set the tone for a dinner party. Consider the elegance of white roses or the simplicity of earthy greenery like ivy. Here are some ideas to help you create a mood — and a beautiful table.

Red Hot

Red is the color of romance, a mood you can achieve with fiery anemones and ranunculuses trimmed short and arranged in brandy snifters. Place one at each setting for bold jolts of color. Other red flowers to consider: geraniums, dahlias, snapdragons, peonies, primroses, cosmos, poppies, tulips and roses.

Blue Note

It's easy to introduce the color of bright skies and deep waters to the table with an arrangement of delphiniums, irises and ageratum in a shapely glass vase lined with large flexible leaves. Others to try include cornflowers, pansies, phlox, morning glories, asters and hydrangea.

◆ ◆ ◆

Olive Focaccia with Pancetta and Onion Topping

◆ ◆ ◆

1³⁄₄ cups (or more) bread flour
1   package fast-rising dry yeast
1   teaspoon sugar
³⁄₄   teaspoon salt
³⁄₄   cup hot water (125°F to 130°F)
2¹⁄₂ tablespoons (or more) olive oil
¹⁄₂   cup chopped pitted Kalamata olives*

Olive oil

2   ounces pancetta or bacon, chopped
1   medium onion, thinly sliced
1¹⁄₂ teaspoons chopped fresh rosemary or ¹⁄₂ teaspoon dried

Combine 1³⁄₄ cups flour, yeast, sugar and salt in processor. Combine ³⁄₄ cup hot water and 1¹⁄₂ tablespoons olive oil in cup. With machine running, pour water mixture into processor through feed tube. Process until dough forms, then continue processing 40 seconds to knead. Add olives and process to combine. Knead dough on floured surface until no longer sticky, adding more flour if necessary.

Grease medium bowl with olive oil. Add dough, turning to coat surface. Cover with towel and let dough rise in warm draft-free area until doubled in volume, about 35 minutes.

Preheat oven to 375°F. Grease 13-inch pizza pan or baking sheet. Punch dough down. Let rest 5 minutes. Roll out to 12-inch round on floured surface. Transfer to prepared pan. Build up edges slightly. Let rise in warm draft-free area 15 minutes. Dimple dough with fingertips and build up edge again. Let rise 15 minutes.

Meanwhile, heat 1 tablespoon olive oil in heavy medium skillet over medium-high heat. Add chopped pancetta, onion and rosemary and sauté until onion just begins to soften, 5 minutes.

Tilt skillet with onion mixture and, with pastry brush, brush bread dough with olive oil in bottom of skillet, using additional olive oil if necessary to coat. Top bread dough with onion mixture. Sprinkle with freshly ground pepper. Bake bread until brown on bottom and edges, about 30 minutes. Cut hot bread into wedges.

*Black brine-cured Kalamata olives are available at Greek and Italian markets and some supermarkets.

MAKES 1 LOAF

Maslin Rolls

♦ ♦ ♦

1/4   cup warm water (105°F to 115°F)
1   package plus ¾ teaspoon dry yeast
1   teaspoon sugar
1⅔ cups milk, room temperature
3   tablespoons vegetable oil
2   teaspoons salt
1   cup whole wheat flour
2   cups (about) bread flour

1½ cups old-fashioned rolled oats
⅔   cup rye flakes*
½   cup toasted wheat germ

   Additional milk
   Additional rye flakes

Combine ¼ cup warm water, yeast and sugar in large bowl. Stir to dissolve yeast. Let mixture stand until foamy, about 10 minutes. Mix in 1⅔ cups milk, vegetable oil and salt. Add 1 cup whole wheat flour and 1½ cups bread flour and stir 2 minutes. Cover dough with plastic wrap; let dough rise in warm draft-free area until puffy, about 30 minutes.

Gradually mix oats, ⅔ cup rye flakes and wheat germ into dough. Mix in enough remaining bread flour to form slightly sticky dough. Knead dough on lightly floured surface until elastic, about 10 minutes. Lightly oil large bowl. Add dough, turning to coat. Cover with plastic. Let rise in warm draft-free area until doubled in volume, about 1 hour.

Lightly grease heavy large baking sheet. Punch down dough. Turn out dough onto lightly floured surface. Divide in half. Cut each half into 5 pieces. Roll each piece into ball. Transfer to prepared baking sheet, spacing evenly. Using scissors, cut cross pattern in top of each dough ball. Cover and let rise in warm draft-free area until almost doubled, about 1 hour.

Preheat oven to 425°F. Brush rolls with milk. Sprinkle with rye flakes. Bake until rolls are brown and sound hollow when tapped on bottom, about 20 minutes. Transfer to rack and cool.

*Available at natural foods stores.

MAKES 10

Summer Whites

An all-white centerpiece is the perfect choice for a sophisticated look. Try mixing roses, stock, ranunculuses and freesias, then arrange them in a silver pedestal bowl.

Naturally Green

Green is ideal for accenting casual and comfortable occasions. To create a vinelike arrangement that sits directly on the table (like the one shown above), choose flowers and greenery that bend easily, then trim stems from blossoms (such as viburnum, unopened lilac and hellebore) and slip them into mini herb jars. Twist greenery such as smilax and ivy around the jars.

♦ ♦ ♦

Selkirk Bannock

◆ ◆ ◆

3   cups (about) bread flour
2   tablespoons sugar
1   package fast-rising dry yeast
$^{1}/_{2}$ teaspoon salt
$^{3}/_{4}$ cup milk
$^{1}/_{2}$ cup (1 stick) unsalted butter

$2^{1}/_{2}$ cups golden raisins

1   egg yolk beaten with 1 tablespoon water (glaze)

Mix $2^{1}/_{2}$ cups flour, sugar, yeast and salt in large bowl. Bring milk and butter to simmer in medium saucepan, stirring until butter melts. Cool to 125°F to 130°F. Stir into dry ingredients. Mix in enough remaining flour to form soft dough. Turn out onto floured surface and knead until smooth and elastic, about 5 minutes. Lightly oil large bowl. Add dough, turning to coat. Cover and let rise in warm draft-free area until doubled in volume, about $1^{1}/_{2}$ hours.

Lightly grease baking sheet. Punch down dough. Knead in raisins. Shape dough into 7-inch-diameter round. Place on prepared sheet. Cover with towel and let rise in warm area until almost doubled in volume, about 40 minutes.

Preheat oven to 375°F. Brush bread with egg glaze. Bake until bread is golden and sounds hollow when tapped on bottom, about 45 minutes. Transfer to rack and cool. *(Can be made 1 day ahead. Wrap tightly; store at room temperature.)*

MAKES 1 LOAF

◆ ◆ ◆

This fruited bread was first made by Robbie Douglas in 1859 at his bakery in the center of Selkirk in the Borders region of Scotland. Within a few years, its fame and popularity had spread, no doubt helped by accounts that Queen Victoria would have nothing more with her tea than a slice of Selkirk Bannock, while on a visit to Sir Walter Scott's granddaughter at nearby Abbotsford.

◆ ◆ ◆

Peppery Grilled Garlic Bread

◆ ◆ ◆

$^{1}/_{2}$ cup (1 stick) unsalted butter, room temperature
3   large garlic cloves, pressed
1   teaspoon ground pepper
1   teaspoon fresh lemon juice

16   1-inch-thick French bread or sourdough baguette slices
$^{1}/_{3}$ cup olive oil

Mix first 4 ingredients in small bowl. Season with salt. *(Can be made ahead. Cover and refrigerate 2 days or freeze 1 month. Bring to room temperature before using.)*

Prepare barbecue (medium-high heat). Lightly brush both sides of bread with oil. Grill until slightly crisp and light brown, about 2 minutes per side. Spread both sides of bread with garlic butter. Serve immediately.

8 SERVINGS

Tuscan Walnut Bread

◆ ◆ ◆

2   cups warm water (105°F to 115°F)
1   envelope dry yeast
1   tablespoon salt
¹⁄₂ cup chopped walnuts
5   cups (about) bread flour

Whisk 2 cups warm water and 1 envelope dry yeast in large bowl until yeast dissolves. Let stand 10 minutes. Mix in salt, then chopped walnuts. Stir in enough flour 1 cup at a time to form dough that is too stiff to stir. Turn out dough onto floured surface and knead in enough remaining flour to form soft, smooth dough. Continue kneading until smooth, elastic and slightly sticky, about 5 minutes. Lightly oil large bowl. Add dough, turning to coat with oil. Cover and let rise in warm draft-free area until doubled in volume, about 1½ hours.

Preheat oven to 350°F. Lightly flour 2 baking sheets. Gently turn out dough onto lightly floured work surface (do not allow dough to deflate). Using long sharp knife, cut dough into 3 equal pieces. Gently stretch each piece into elongated loaf shape (do not allow dough to deflate). Transfer to prepared baking sheets, spacing 2 inches apart. Bake until loaves sound hollow when tapped on bottom, about 1 hour. Transfer loaves to rack and cool completely. *(Can be prepared 2 weeks ahead. Wrap tightly and freeze. Thaw before serving.)*

MAKES 3 LOAVES

◆ ◆ ◆

Handle this bread dough carefully: It has only one rising and is quite soft to work with.

◆ ◆ ◆

THE KITCHEN PANTRY

The pantry is central to every kitchen. It's the room's main storage place, where canned and dry goods are kept along with other nonperishables and culinary miscellanea. And it can take shape in any number of ways, from a walk-in "closet" to a couple of cabinets along a wall. When planning your pantry, here are some designs to keep in mind.

Walk-in Pantry

For many, this is the ideal pantry — if there's room in the kitchen for it. This type offers space for more than just food, everything from tableware to pots and pans, wine and books.

◆ ◆ ◆

Sunflower Pumpkin Bread

◆ ◆ ◆

2½ cups all purpose flour
2 cups sugar
2 teaspoons baking soda
½ teaspoon ground cinnamon
½ teaspoon ground ginger
½ teaspoon ground allspice
½ teaspoon salt
1½ cups canned solid pack pumpkin
½ cup vegetable oil
½ cup shelled sunflower seeds
½ cup finely chopped walnuts

Preheat oven to 350°F. Butter and flour two 8½ x 4½ x 2½-inch loaf pans. Combine first 7 ingredients in medium bowl. Mix pumpkin, oil, sunflower seeds and walnuts in large bowl. Stir dry ingredients into pumpkin mixture (batter will be thick). Divide batter between prepared pans. Bake until tester inserted into centers comes out clean, about 55 minutes. Cool breads in pans on racks 10 minutes. Turn out breads onto racks and cool completely. *(Can be made 1 day ahead. Wrap tightly and store at room temperature.)* Cut bread into slices and serve.

MAKES 2 LOAVES

Chocolate Chip and Orange Muffins

◆ ◆ ◆

3 cups all purpose flour
1¼ cups sugar
2 teaspoons baking powder
1¼ cups milk
¾ cup vegetable oil
2 large eggs
4 teaspoons grated orange peel
1 12-ounce package semisweet chocolate chips

Preheat oven to 350°F. Line ½-cup muffin cups with foil liners. Combine flour, sugar and baking powder in large bowl. Make well in center of flour mixture. In another bowl, mix milk, oil, eggs and orange peel. Stir milk mixture into dry ingredients (mixture will be lumpy). Add chocolate chips to batter. Divide batter among muffin cups. Bake muffins until tester inserted into center comes out clean, about 20 minutes. Transfer muffins to rack. Serve warm or at room temperature.

MAKES 18

Pecan Muffins

◆ ◆ ◆

1³/₄ cups sifted all purpose flour
¹/₂ cup sugar
1 teaspoon baking powder
¹/₂ teaspoon baking soda
¹/₂ teaspoon salt
¹/₂ cup sour cream
¹/₂ cup peach preserves
1 egg
1 teaspoon vanilla extract
²/₃ cup chopped pecans, toasted

Position rack in center of oven and preheat to 400°F. Line 10 muffin cups with muffin papers.

Sift first 5 ingredients into large bowl. Whisk sour cream, preserves, egg and vanilla to blend in medium bowl. Add sour cream mixture and pecans to dry ingredients and stir just until combined; do not overmix.

Divide batter among muffin cups. Bake until tester inserted into center of muffins comes out clean, about 20 minutes. Cool 15 minutes before serving.

MAKES 10

In this design, tall swing-out doors are lined with shelves that are just wide enough for single rows of bottles and cans. Inside, U-shaped shelves on top provide easily accessible storage, and on the bottom, pullout drawers offer deeper space.

Upright Pullout Pantry

Instead of shelves that go deep into the wall, this innovative, space-efficient design has them pull out, making it easy to see everything in the wire-rack shelving from two sides. Bottom drawers provide storage for pots and pans.

Lazy Susan Pantry

Sometimes the oldest ideas are the best. The classic lazy Susan is transformed into a multi-tiered pantry for a very narrow opening. Spinning shelves ensure complete visibility and accessibility, and a deep wire basket at the bottom is great for storing vegetables, such as onions.

◆ ◆ ◆

◆ Desserts ◆

There are desserts, and then there are desserts, if you know what we mean. There are homespun fruit crisps, perfect after a hearty supper. There are traditional cookies, just what the kids want when they get in from school. Then there are the big desserts, the ones you save for special occasions, like birthdays. And since both play a part in the pages of *Bon Appétit*, you'll find both here, from the simple to the sublime.

If the fruit crisp idea appeals, try the Bourbon Brown Betty à la Mode on page 177, or maybe the Plum-Peach Crisp on page 181. The cookie monsters in your house will be sure to like the chocolate chip version on page 219. But if it's a birthday tune you're humming, consider the Chocolate-Sour Cream Layer Cake on page 185. Many happy returns. (And may you find yourself happily returning to these pages throughout the year.)

From top: Caramel-Apple Puff Pastry Pie, page 166; Apple Pie with Oatmeal-Pecan Topping, page 172; Apple Butter Swirl Ice Cream Pie with Maple Apples, page 212; Apple Custard Pie with Almonds, page 168; Foursquare Apple-Mince Pie, page 162.

✦ PIES & TARTS ✦

Lemon-Nutmeg Pie Crust Dough

◆ ◆ ◆

2 ⅓ *cups unbleached all purpose flour*
1   *tablespoon sugar*
1   *teaspoon salt*
1   *teaspoon grated lemon peel*
½   *teaspoon ground nutmeg*
½   *cup (1 stick) chilled unsalted butter, cut into ½-inch pieces*
½   *cup chilled solid vegetable shortening, cut into ½-inch pieces*
3   *tablespoons water*
1   *tablespoon fresh lemon juice*

Combine first 5 ingredients in processor. Add butter and short-ening and blend until mixture resembles coarse meal. Add 3 table-spoons water and 1 tablespoon fresh lemon juice and process until moist clumps form. Gather dough into 2 balls; flatten balls into disks. Wrap each disk in plastic and refrigerate 30 minutes.

MAKES ENOUGH FOR 2 CRUSTS

Foursquare Apple-Mince Pies

◆ ◆ ◆

Lemon-Nutmeg Pie Crust Dough (see recipe above)

2   *small pippin apples (about 10 ounces), peeled, cored, chopped*
⅔   *cup purchased mincemeat*
2   *tablespoons firmly packed golden brown sugar*
1   *tablespoon unsalted butter, cut into pieces*
½   *teaspoon ground cinnamon*
½   *teaspoon grated lemon peel*
     Pinch of ground cloves
     Pinch of ground black pepper

1   *large egg*
1   *tablespoon milk*

Preheat oven to 400°F. Line large cookie sheet with parch-ment. Roll out 1 dough disk on floured surface to ¼-inch-thick square. Cut into four 4½-inch squares. Transfer to cookie sheet.

Combine apples, mincemeat, sugar, butter, cinnamon, lemon peel, cloves and pepper in large bowl. Spoon ¼ of filling onto center of each pastry square, leaving ½-inch border on all 4 sides. Brush borders lightly with water. Roll out second dough disk to scant ¼-inch-thick square. Cut into four 5-inch squares. Place one 5-inch square over filling on each 4½-inch square. Press edges together to seal. Crimp edges with fork. Cut X or small design in top of pies.

Beat egg and milk in small bowl to blend. Brush top of pies with egg mixture. Bake until crusts are golden brown and apples are tender, about 30 minutes. Serve warm.

MAKES 4

Vanilla Cream and Apricot Tart

◆ ◆ ◆

½   *vanilla bean, cut into ½-inch pieces*
½   *cup sugar*
8   *ounces cream cheese, room temperature*
1   *tablespoon whipping cream*
1   *tablespoon sour cream*
2   *tablespoons plus 4 teaspoons sweet Marsala wine*

1   *All Ready Pie Crust (½ 15-ounce package), room temperature*

½   *cup apricot preserves*
2   *pounds apricots, pitted, thinly sliced*

Coarsely chop vanilla bean in processor. Add sugar and process until vanilla bean is finely ground. Sift sugar through strainer to remove large pieces of vanilla bean. Blend sugar, cream cheese, cream, sour cream and 2 tablespoons Marsala in processor until smooth. Refrigerate while preparing crust.

Preheat oven to 450°F. Roll out crust on lightly floured surface to 13-inch-diameter round. Transfer to 11-inch-diameter tart pan with removable bottom. Pierce all over with fork. Bake until golden, about 16 minutes. Cool completely on rack.

Stir preserves and remaining 4 teaspoons Marsala in heavy small saucepan over medium heat until preserves melt. Brush some preserves thinly over crust. Fill with cream cheese mixture. Top with apricots. Brush apricots with remaining preserves. Refrigerate at least 1 hour. *(Can be prepared 6 hours ahead.)*

8 TO 10 SERVINGS

A PROPER TEA

We have Anna, the seventh Duchess of Bedford, to thank for the tradition of afternoon tea, a national passion with the British since the eighteenth century. In more recent times, the tradition of tea has been discovered by Americans as a civilized way to entertain friends, conduct business, honor graduates and toast brides and mothers-to-be.

The Menu

In addition to scones and a selection of jams, offer finger sandwiches, perhaps cream cheese and walnut or cucumber and watercress. You could also serve slices of a fruit bread. Dessert could be as simple as fresh strawberries or as decadent as flourless chocolate cake.

The Setting

The table set for tea, with its china cups and saucers, plates and silver spoons, is so pretty that it doesn't need much in the way of enhancement. But a bit of gilding never hurts, especially when the occasion is a special one. Line a silver tea tray with doilies and decorate it with flowers and greenery. Tie the flatware with ribbons; set out lace-trimmed napkins. Add a colorful bouquet of fresh spring flowers — arranged in another teapot.

◆ ◆ ◆

Chocolate-Orange Pecan Pie

◆ ◆ ◆

1½ cups all purpose flour
¼ teaspoon (generous) salt
6 tablespoons (¾ stick) chilled unsalted butter, cut into pieces
3 tablespoons chilled solid vegetable shortening
3 tablespoons (about) ice water

1 cup lightly packed dark brown sugar
3 large eggs
¼ cup light corn syrup
2 tablespoons dark rum
1 tablespoon unsalted butter, melted
1 teaspoon grated orange peel
⅛ teaspoon salt
6 ounces bittersweet (not unsweetened) or semisweet chocolate, chopped

2 cups pecan halves, lightly toasted

FOR CRUST: Place flour and ¼ teaspoon salt in large bowl. Add 6 tablespoons butter and shortening and rub with fingertips until mixture resembles coarse meal. Gradually mix in enough water until dough forms moist clumps. Gather into ball; flatten into disk. Wrap in plastic; chill 30 minutes.

Preheat oven to 425°F. Roll out dough on lightly floured surface to 14-inch round. Transfer to 9-inch-diameter glass pie dish. Trim and crimp edges. Freeze 10 minutes. Line with foil; fill with dried beans or pie weights. Bake until sides are set, about 12 minutes. Remove foil and beans and bake crust until pale golden, piercing with toothpick if crust bubbles, about 7 minutes more. Transfer crust to rack. Reduce oven temperature to 350°F.

FOR FILLING: Whisk brown sugar and next 6 ingredients in large bowl. Melt chocolate in top of double boiler over simmering water, stirring until smooth. Whisk chocolate into filling.

Arrange pecan halves in bottom of pie crust. Spoon filling over. Bake until filling puffs and no longer moves in center when pie is shaken, about 30 minutes. Transfer pie to rack and cool completely. *(Pie can be prepared 1 day ahead. Cover and let stand at room temperature.)* Cut pie into wedges and serve.

8 SERVINGS

◆ ◆ ◆

That most famous of all the decadent southern desserts, pecan pie, is made richer and sweeter still with the addition of chocolate. Grated orange peel adds its own special flavor.

◆ ◆ ◆

Maple Sugar Pie

◆ ◆ ◆

1½ cups plus 1 tablespoon all purpose flour

2½ tablespoons sugar

¼ teaspoon salt

10 tablespoons (1¼ sticks) chilled unsalted butter, cut into pieces

4 tablespoons (about) ice water

1 cup golden brown sugar

3 tablespoons unsalted butter, room temperature

3 large eggs, separated, room temperature

1 cup plus 3 tablespoons pure maple syrup

½ cup milk

¾ cup chilled whipping cream
    Leaf-shaped maple sugar candies*

5 large oranges, sliced into rounds (optional)

FOR CRUST: Combine flour, 2½ tablespoons sugar and salt in processor. Add 10 tablespoons butter; blend in using on/off turns until mixture resembles coarse meal. Blend in enough water by table-spoons until dough begins to clump together. Gather into ball; flatten into disk. Wrap in plastic; chill 30 minutes.

Roll out dough on floured surface to 13-inch round. Transfer to 10-inch-diameter pie dish. Trim and crimp edges.

FOR FILLING: Preheat oven to 375°F. Using electric mixer, beat 1 cup sugar, 3 tablespoons butter and yolks in large bowl to blend. Beat in 1 cup syrup and milk. Using electric mixer fitted with clean dry beaters, beat whites in medium bowl until stiff but not dry. Fold beaten egg whites into syrup mixture.

Pour filling into pie shell. Bake until pie is set around edges but center still moves slightly when pan is shaken, about 1 hour (if edges begin to brown too quickly, cover loosely with foil). Cool completely. *(Can be made 8 hours ahead. Let stand at room temperature.)*

Beat cream and 3 tablespoons syrup in medium bowl to medium-stiff peaks. Spoon cream into pastry bag fitted with medium star tip. Pipe cream around top edge of pie. Garnish with maple candies. Serve with orange slices, if desired.

*Available at specialty foods stores and many candy shops.

10 SERVINGS

Caramel-Apple Puff Pastry Pie

❖ ❖ ❖

2¼ cups unbleached all purpose flour

1 teaspoon salt

10 tablespoons (1¼ sticks) unsalted butter, room temperature

6 tablespoons water

10 tablespoons (1¼ sticks) chilled unsalted butter

2 tablespoons (¼ stick) unsalted butter

½ cup plus 3 tablespoons sugar

4 large Golden Delicious apples (about 2¾ pounds), peeled, cut into ⅓-inch-thick slices

¾ cup unsweetened applesauce

½ teaspoon vanilla extract

1 large egg, beaten to blend (glaze)

FOR PASTRY: Combine flour and salt in large bowl. Add 10 tablespoons butter and cut in, using pastry blender or fingers, until mixture resembles coarse meal. Stir in water with fork. Knead gently with fingertips just until smooth dough forms. Shape into rectangle, wrap in plastic and refrigerate 1 hour.

Cut 10 tablespoons chilled butter into 9 even pieces. Arrange pieces side by side on waxed paper, forming square. Cover with second sheet of waxed paper. Pound butter several times with rolling pin to make butter more pliable. Peel off waxed paper. Break butter into small pieces.

Roll out dough on lightly floured surface to 9 x 5-inch rectangle. Turn dough so that 1 short side faces you. Place butter pieces evenly atop lower 6 inches of dough. Fold unbuttered 3 inches of dough over half of buttered dough. Fold remaining 3 inches of buttered dough over, folding as for letter. Roll out to 12 x 18-inch rectangle. Fold short sides over to meet in center, then fold in half in same direction, forming approximately 12 x 4½-inch rectangle. Repeat rolling to 12 x 18-inch rectangle and folding to 12 x 4½-inch rectangle. Wrap in plastic and chill. *(Can be made 3 days ahead. Keep refrigerated.)*

FOR FILLING: Melt 2 tablespoons butter in heavy large skillet over medium-high heat. Add ½ cup sugar and stir until moistened with butter. Cook until sugar melts and turns deep amber color, stirring occasionally, about 4 minutes. Add apples and sauté until golden brown and tender and no liquid remains in skillet, about 15 minutes. Cool. Stir applesauce, vanilla and 2 tablespoons sugar into apples in skillet.

❖ ❖ ❖

The crust for this pie is called "rough puff pastry," a cross between real puff pastry and a pie crust. If you're short on time, use purchased frozen puff pastry sheets.

❖ ❖ ❖

Cut dough in half. Let dough stand at room temperature until slightly softened, about 15 minutes. Roll out each piece to 12-inch square. Trim edges evenly. Transfer squares to 2 heavy ungreased cookie sheets. Chill 15 minutes.

Preheat oven to 425°F. Pierce squares all over with fork. Spread filling evenly over 1 square, leaving 1¼-inch border. Brush border with water. Place second square atop filling and press edges to seal. Brush with glaze. Sprinkle with 1 tablespoon sugar. Bake until golden brown, about 30 minutes. Cool until warm. Cut square into 4 squares. Cut each square diagonally in half and serve immediately.

8 SERVINGS

"Très Vite" Apple Tarts

◆ ◆ ◆

2   large Golden Delicious apples, peeled, cored, thinly sliced
2   tablespoons fresh lemon juice
1½ teaspoons vanilla extract
1   egg
1   tablespoon milk
¼   cup sugar
½   teaspoon ground cinnamon

1   frozen puff pastry sheet (half 17¼-ounce package), thawed

¼   cup apricot preserves
     Sliced almonds (optional)
     Whipped cream (optional)

Preheat oven to 350°F. Mix apples, lemon juice and 1 teaspoon vanilla in medium bowl. Beat egg and milk together in small bowl. Mix sugar and cinnamon in another small bowl.

Roll out pastry on floured surface to 10-inch square. Cut into four 5-inch squares. Brush squares with egg mixture. Place on ungreased baking sheet. Drain apples. Overlap apples atop pastry, leaving ¼-inch border around edges. Sprinkle apples and pastry edges with cinnamon mixture. Bake until brown, about 30 minutes.

Combine preserves and ½ teaspoon vanilla in small saucepan. Stir over low heat until melted and smooth. Brush glaze over apples. Sprinkle with almonds if desired. Serve warm or at room temperature with whipped cream, if desired.

4 SERVINGS

◆ ◆ ◆

True puff pastry, or *pâte feuilletée*, is one of the most difficult things to make in the classic French repertoire. To give you an idea, here's how the *Joy of Cooking* puts it: "To become an amateur champion, keep in mind first and foremost that this most delicate and challenging of pastries must be made the way porcupines make love — that is, very, very carefully."

To spare you the effort, frozen puff pastry, available in supermarkets across the country, is an excellent alternative. Here, it makes this lovely dessert "very fast" to prepare.

◆ ◆ ◆

Apple Custard Pie with Almonds

❖ ❖ ❖

$^3/_4$ cup unbleached all purpose flour

$^1/_2$ cup sliced almonds

1   tablespoon sugar

$^1/_4$ teaspoon salt

6   tablespoons ($^3/_4$ stick) chilled unsalted butter, cut into $^1/_2$-inch pieces

$1^1/_2$ tablespoons water

$^1/_8$ teaspoon almond extract

2   tablespoons ($^1/_4$ stick) unsalted butter

3   Gala or Golden Delicious apples (about $1^1/_4$ pounds), peeled, cored, cut into 1-inch chunks

2   tablespoons Calvados or brandy

$1^1/_4$ cups whipping cream

1   2-inch piece vanilla bean, split lengthwise

4   large egg yolks

$^1/_4$ cup sugar

1   large egg

3   tablespoons sliced almonds

FOR CRUST: Combine first 4 ingredients in processor and blend until almonds are finely ground. Add 6 tablespoons butter and process until mixture resembles coarse meal. Combine water and almond extract in small bowl. Add to processor and blend until moist clumps form. Gather dough into ball; flatten ball into disk. Chill 30 minutes.

Roll out dough between sheets of waxed paper to 12-inch round. Peel off top sheet of paper. Invert dough into 9-inch-diameter glass pie dish. Peel off paper. Press dough into dish (dough is fragile; press with finger to patch any holes). Trim dough, leaving $^1/_2$-inch overhang. Fold edge under and crimp decoratively. Freeze crust 30 minutes.

Preheat oven to 400°F. Line crust with foil. Fill with dried beans or pie weights. Bake until crust is set, about 20 minutes. Remove foil and beans; continue baking until crust is golden brown, about 10 minutes longer. Cool.

FOR FILLING: Preheat oven to 325°F. Melt 2 tablespoons butter in heavy large skillet over medium-low heat. Add apples and sauté until tender, about 15 minutes. Using slotted spoon, transfer apples to plate. Increase heat to medium-high, add Calvados to skillet and boil until reduced to glaze, about 1 minute. Add cream to skillet. Scrape seeds from vanilla bean into cream; add bean and bring to

❖ ❖ ❖

For this dessert, a rich vanilla custard enhanced with Calvados (an apple brandy from France) and chunks of apple is showcased in a delicate almond crust.

❖ ❖ ❖

boil. Beat 4 egg yolks and sugar in heavy medium saucepan to blend. Gradually whisk in hot cream mixture. Stir over low heat until mixture thickens slightly and coats back of spoon, about 7 minutes; do not boil. Remove from heat; whisk in 1 whole egg.

Place apples in crust. Pour custard over apples. Sprinkle custard with almonds. Bake until custard is set in center and slightly puffed around edges, about 35 minutes. Cool completely.

6 TO 8 SERVINGS

Almond Cheesecake Fruit Tart

◆ ◆ ◆

³/₄ cup all purpose flour
¹/₄ cup sliced almonds
1 tablespoon sugar
¹/₄ teaspoon salt
7 tablespoons chilled unsalted butter, cut into pieces
¹/₂ tablespoon (about) cold water

1 cup sliced almonds
¹/₃ cup sugar
1 8-ounce package cream cheese, room temperature
2 large eggs
¹/₄ teaspoon almond extract
Assorted fresh fruit (such as strawberries, blueberries and sliced kiwi fruit)

FOR CRUST: Blend first 4 ingredients in processor until nuts are finely ground. Add butter and cut in using on/off turns until mixture resembles coarse meal. Add water and blend until dough begins to clump together. Gather dough into ball; flatten into disk. Wrap in plastic and chill 20 minutes. *(Can be made 2 days ahead.)*

Roll out dough on lightly floured surface to 11-inch round. Transfer to 9-inch-diameter tart pan with removable bottom. Press dough evenly into pan; trim edges. Freeze crust 30 minutes.

Preheat oven to 425°F. Bake crust until golden, about 15 minutes. Cool. Reduce oven temperature to 325°F.

FOR FILLING: Finely grind almonds and sugar in processor. Add cream cheese and blend until smooth. Add eggs and almond extract and blend using on/off turns. Spoon mixture into crust. Bake until filling is set, about 18 minutes. Cool completely. *(Can be prepared 6 hours ahead. Cover loosely.)* Arrange fruit atop tart.

6 SERVINGS

NAPKINS: CREATIVE FOLDS

A seemingly minor detail, like the way a napkin is folded, can do a lot for your table, especially if you want to add interest to an informal setting. Here are some simple ideas to try:

◆ Tie two napkins together with raffia for a generous, welcoming effect. Tuck in fresh bittersweet berries, evergreen sprigs, chive blossoms or flowers.

◆ Use a napkin as gift wrap for a small, framed, handwritten copy of the evening's menu. Add a length of ribbon or twine to finish the package off.

◆ Napkin "pockets," which hold flatware, are terrific for buffet tables. Make them by folding a napkin into a square with the four free corners at the upper left. Fold the upper left point of the top layer down to the right corner. Fold under the top right and bottom left corners. Tuck in flatware.

◆ ◆ ◆

Raspberry-Almond Truffle Tart

◆ ◆ ◆

◆ ◆ ◆

Here, almonds flavor the crust of a chocolate-raspberry tart. If you can get golden raspberries, use some of them for color contrast.

◆ ◆ ◆

$^1/_2$ cup blanched slivered almonds
5 tablespoons sugar
$^1/_4$ teaspoon vanilla extract
$^1/_8$ teaspoon almond extract
1 cup all purpose flour
$^1/_4$ teaspoon salt
9 tablespoons chilled unsalted butter, cut into pieces
3 tablespoons (about) ice water

$^1/_2$ cup red currant jelly
2 teaspoons sugar

6 ounces bittersweet (not unsweetened) or semisweet chocolate, chopped
2 tablespoons ($^1/_4$ stick) unsalted butter
$^2/_3$ cup whipping cream

2 $^1/_2$-pint baskets fresh raspberries
   Bittersweet chocolate shavings
   Powdered sugar

FOR CRUST: Combine first 4 ingredients in processor. Process using on/off turns until almonds are finely chopped. Add flour and salt and blend until mixed. Add 9 tablespoons butter and cut in using on/off turns until mixture resembles coarse meal. Mix in enough water until dough begins to clump together. Gather dough into ball; flatten into disk. Wrap in plastic and refrigerate 30 minutes.

Position rack in center of oven and preheat to 400°F. Roll out dough on lightly floured surface to 13-inch round. Fold dough in half. Transfer to 9-inch-diameter tart pan with removable sides. Unfold dough. Trim edges, leaving $^1/_4$-inch border. Fold border over to form thick sides. Press dough against sides of tart pan. Freeze 10 minutes.

Pierce bottom of dough all over with fork. Bake until golden, piercing with toothpick if crust bubbles and pressing up sides with back of fork if slipping, about 25 minutes. Transfer to rack; cool.

FOR FILLING: Simmer jelly and sugar in heavy small saucepan until slightly thickened, stirring constantly, about 2 minutes. Brush inside of crust with about $1^1/_2$ tablespoons jelly mixture.

Place 6 ounces chocolate and 2 tablespoons butter in medium metal bowl. Bring cream to simmer in small saucepan. Pour over chocolate mixture; let stand 1 minute. Stir chocolate mixture until melted and smooth. Pour into crust. Chill until filling is set, at least 4 hours or overnight.

Starting at edge, arrange berries in circles atop tart. Rewarm jelly mixture; brush over berries. *(Can be made 1 day ahead; chill.)*

Sprinkle chocolate shavings in center of tart. Lightly sift powdered sugar over chocolate shavings. Remove pan sides.

12 SERVINGS

Chocolate and Berry Tart

◆ ◆ ◆

1   *frozen puff pastry sheet, thawed (half of 17¼-ounce package)*
1   *egg beaten with 1 tablespoon water (glaze)*
    Sugar

3   *ounces bittersweet (not unsweetened) or semisweet chocolate, chopped*
1   *tablespoon plus ¼ cup currant jelly*
2   *tablespoons plus ¼ cup sour cream*

¾   *cup raspberries*
¾   *cup blueberries*

2   *teaspoons crème de cassis liqueur (optional)*

Preheat oven to 350°F. Roll out pastry on floured surface to 14 x 11-inch rectangle. Trim two 1-inch-wide strips off each edge (for a total of 8 strips) and reserve. Transfer pastry rectangle to ungreased baking sheet. Pierce rectangle all over with fork. Brush with glaze. Arrange 1 pastry strip atop each edge of rectangle, trimming to join strips at corners. Brush with glaze. Top each edge with remaining pastry strips, covering corner seams and trimming to square off. Brush with glaze. Sprinkle with sugar. Bake 5 minutes. Pierce pastry rectangle (not sides) all over with fork. Continue baking until golden, about 20 minutes longer. Cool on rack.

Melt chocolate in top of double boiler over simmering water, stirring until smooth. Add 1 tablespoon jelly; stir until melted. Add 2 tablespoons sour cream; mix until smooth. Spread in crust.

Melt remaining ¼ cup jelly in small saucepan over low heat, stirring often. Combine berries in bowl. Add melted jelly; stir to coat. Immediately spoon berries atop soft chocolate in crust, covering chocolate completely. Chill just until set, about 1 hour.

Combine ¼ cup sour cream and crème de cassis. Serve with tart.

4 SERVINGS

The smell of cinnamon fills the air in the island nation of Sri Lanka, particularly in the Southwest, a region covered with plantations of the tree called *Cinnamomum zeylanicum*. The bark of its branches is harvested to become the cinnamon that connoisseurs consider the world's finest.

In the wild, cinnamon trees can grow as tall as 50 feet. In contrast, cultivated trees are kept pruned to eight-foot-tall bushes, which keeps the shoots narrow and easily accessible and the bark thin and tender. At harvest time, the two-year-old shoots are cut and taken to a processing center. The outer bark is carefully scraped away, and the paper-thin inner bark is peeled off. This inner bark rolls naturally into quills.

While Sri Lanka exports an average of about seven thousand tons of cinnamon per year, little of that ever reaches the United States. Americans, it seems, have developed a taste for the more pungent type of cinnamon know as cassia. If you wish to sample the true Sri Lanka cinnamon, you'll have to purchase it from a spice shop.

◆ ◆ ◆

Apple Pie with Oatmeal-Pecan Topping

◆ ◆ ◆

1   cup unbleached all purpose flour
2   tablespoons firmly packed golden brown sugar
½   teaspoon salt
½   teaspoon ground cinnamon
¼   cup (½ stick) chilled unsalted butter, cut into ½-inch pieces
¼   cup solid vegetable shortening
¼   cup old-fashioned oats
1   tablespoon water

5   pippin apples (about 2 pounds), peeled, cored, thinly sliced
¼   cup sugar
1   tablespoon unbleached all purpose flour
1   teaspoon ground cinnamon

½   cup unbleached all purpose flour
¼   cup firmly packed golden brown sugar
1   teaspoon ground cinnamon
¼   teaspoon salt
6   tablespoons (¾ stick) chilled unsalted butter, cut into ½-inch pieces
½   cup old-fashioned oats
3   tablespoons chopped pecans

Vanilla ice cream

FOR CRUST: Combine first 4 ingredients in processor. Add ¼ cup butter and shortening and process until mixture resembles coarse meal. Add ¼ cup oats and pulse to blend. Mix in water and process until moist clumps form. Gather dough into ball; flatten ball into disk. Wrap in plastic and refrigerate 30 minutes. *(Can be prepared 3 days ahead. Keep refrigerated. Let dough soften slightly at room temperature before continuing.)*

FOR FILLING: Position rack in lowest third of oven and preheat to 400°F. Combine apples and next 3 ingredients in large bowl and toss well. Set aside.

FOR TOPPING: Combine ½ cup flour, ¼ cup brown sugar, 1 teaspoon cinnamon and ¼ teaspoon salt in processor. Add 6 tablespoons butter and process until mixture forms small moist clumps. Mix in ½ cup oats and 3 tablespoons pecans.

Roll out dough disk between sheets of waxed paper to 11-inch round. Peel off top sheet of paper. Invert dough into 9-inch-diameter glass pie dish. Peel off paper. Press dough into dish (dough is fragile; press with finger to patch any holes). Trim dough, leaving ½-inch overhang. Fold edge under and crimp decoratively. Spoon filling into crust. Sprinkle topping over filling.

Bake pie until crust and topping are golden brown, apples are tender and juices bubble thickly, covering edges with foil after 20 minutes, about 55 minutes. Cool slightly. Serve with vanilla ice cream.

6 SERVINGS

Berry Napoleons

◆ ◆ ◆

1   *frozen puff pastry sheet (half of 17¼-ounce package), thawed*
1   *egg beaten with 1 teaspoon milk (glaze)*
2   *teaspoons sugar*
½   *teaspoon ground cardamom*

1   *10-ounce package frozen raspberries in syrup, thawed*
½   *1-pint basket strawberries, sliced*

Vanilla frozen yogurt

Preheat oven to 375°F. Roll out pastry on lightly floured surface to 12-inch square. Cut out two 4 x 5-inch rectangles and transfer to ungreased cookie sheet (reserve remaining pastry for another use). Brush pastries with glaze. Mix sugar and ¼ teaspoon cardamom and sprinkle over pastries. Bake until puffed and brown, about 20 minutes. Transfer to rack and cool.

Drain syrup from raspberries into heavy small saucepan. Boil until thickened slightly, about 4 minutes. Combine raspberries and sliced strawberries in small bowl. Add reduced syrup and remaining ¼ teaspoon cardamom. *(Berry mixture can be prepared 2 hours ahead. Cover and refrigerate.)*

Split each pastry into 2 layers. Place bottoms on plates. Layer with frozen yogurt, some of berry mixture, then pastry tops. Spoon a few berries atop each pastry and serve.

2 SERVINGS

◆ ◆ ◆

Elegance just doesn't come any easier than this pretty treat made with purchased puff pastry.

◆ ◆ ◆

Plum Napoleon with
Orange Sabayon Sauce

♦ ♦ ♦

3   frozen puff pastry sheets (one and one-half 17¼-ounce packages), thawed

4   large egg yolks
¼   cup sugar
    Pinch of salt
¼   cup orange juice
2   tablespoons Grand Marnier or other orange liqueur
½   cup chilled whipping cream

2½ pounds plums, pitted, thinly sliced
½   cup sugar
¾   teaspoon fresh lemon juice
    Pinch of salt
3   tablespoons unsalted butter

Position rack in center of oven and preheat to 375°F. Roll out 1 pastry sheet on floured surface to 10-inch square. Cut out four 4 x 5-inch rectangles. Place pastries on baking sheet. Pierce all over with fork. Freeze 10 minutes. Set metal cooling rack over pastries and bake until crisp and brown, about 20 minutes. Carefully lift off rack, revealing design. Transfer pastries to rack; cool. Repeat cutting and baking of remaining pastry sheets, forming 12 pastries. *(Can be made 6 hours ahead. Let stand at room temperature.)*

FOR SABAYON: Using electric mixer, beat yolks, ¼ cup sugar and pinch of salt in large stainless steel bowl just until combined. Beat in orange juice and Grand Marnier. Place bowl over large saucepan of boiling water and beat at high speed until sabayon is thick enough to mound and thermometer inserted into sabayon resisters 160°F, about 5 minutes. Place bowl over larger bowl filled with ice and water and beat sabayon at very low speed until cool, about 2 minutes. Beat cream in medium bowl until firm peaks form. Fold cream into sabayon in 2 additions. *(Can be prepared 3 hours ahead. Cover and chill.)*

FOR FILLING: Combine plums, ½ cup sugar, lemon juice and pinch of salt in heavy large skillet. Cook over medium-high heat 5 minutes, stirring occasionally. Add butter and cook until plums are soft but still retain shape, stirring occasionally, about 5 minutes.

Place 1 pastry rectangle, design side up, on each of 6 plates. Spoon filling over each. Mound sabayon over. Top each with pastry.

6 SERVINGS

♦ ♦ ♦

The classic French dessert gets a summertime twist with the addition of fresh fruit to the filling. Using purchased puff pastry makes this version easy to prepare. Set a metal cooling rack on the pastry as it bakes to create a pretty design on the top. Dust with powdered sugar, if you like.

♦ ♦ ♦

Plum Napoleon with Orange Sabayon Sauce; Plum Raspberry Sorbet, page 213.

Poached Pears with Cranberry-Cardamom Sauce

♦ ♦ ♦

2   *cups dry white wine*
1   *cup cranberries*
$^{1}/_{2}$ *cup plus 3 tablespoons sugar*
$^{1}/_{2}$ *cup water*
3   *whole cloves*
2   *2 x 1-inch orange peel strips*
$^{1}/_{2}$ *teaspoon (generous) ground cardamom*
2   *firm but ripe pears, peeled*

    Vanilla frozen yogurt
    Almond cookies

Combine first 7 ingredients in heavy medium saucepan. Bring to boil, stirring to dissolve sugar. Add pears, reduce heat, cover and simmer until tender when pierced with knife, turning once, about 20 minutes. Transfer pears to bowl using slotted spoon. Chill.

Boil poaching liquid until reduced to 1 cup plus 2 tablespoons, stirring occasionally, about 15 minutes. Strain into bowl, pressing on solids. Rewarm sauce over medium-low heat. Stand pears on plates. Place scoop of frozen yogurt next to each pear. Drizzle sauce over pears and yogurt. Serve with cookies.

2 SERVINGS

Dried Fruit and Fresh Grapefruit Compote

♦ ♦ ♦

3   *cups cranberry or cranberry-apple juice*
4   *ounces dried apricots*
4   *ounces dried pears*
4   *ounces dried peaches*
6   *tablespoons honey*
6   *whole allspice berries*

2   *grapefruit*

Combine first 6 ingredients in heavy medium saucepan. Simmer until fruit is tender, about 10 minutes. Transfer fruit to medium bowl using slotted spoon. Boil poaching liquid until syrupy, about 5 minutes. Pour syrup over fruit. Refrigerate until well chilled.

Cut all peel and white pith from grapefruit. Working over bowl to catch juices, cut between membranes to remove sections. Add grapefruit to bowl. *(Can be made 2 days ahead. Cover poached fruit and grapefruit separately and chill.)* Drain grapefruit sections, reserving juice, and add to poached fruit. Thin syrup with grapefruit juice if desired and serve.

6 SERVINGS

Bourbon Brown Betty à la Mode

◆ ◆ ◆

⅓   cup water
⅓   cup bourbon
⅓   cup golden raisins
1   teaspoon vanilla extract

2 ½ *pounds tart green apples, peeled, cored, cut into* ½-inch *chunks*
⅓   cup sugar
2   cups fresh whole grain breadcrumbs
6   tablespoons (¾ stick) unsalted butter, melted
¼   cup firmly packed brown sugar
½   teaspoon ground cinnamon

Vanilla ice cream

Bring first 2 ingredients to boil in medium saucepan. Add golden raisins and vanilla; remove from heat, cover and let stand until cool, about 1 hour.

Preheat oven to 375°F. Transfer raisins with soaking liquid to large bowl. Add apples and ⅓ cup sugar; toss well. Mix breadcrumbs, butter, brown sugar and cinnamon in medium bowl. Spoon half of apples into 8-inch square glass baking dish. Top with half of breadcrumbs. Repeat layering with apples and breadcrumbs.

Bake until apples are tender and topping is crisp and brown, about 55 minutes. Transfer to rack; cool 15 minutes. Spoon into bowls. Top with ice cream.

6 SERVINGS

◆ ◆ ◆

The "brown" is taken literally in this recipe, with whole grain bread used for the breadcrumbs; it produces a crunchy topping. But never fear: Bourbon-plumped raisins and scoops of vanilla ice cream will dispel any health food notions those fiber-filled crumbs may give.

Cheese Blintzes with Blueberry Sauce

◆ ◆ ◆

1   *32-ounce container large curd cottage cheese (do not use low-fat or nonfat)*

2   *large eggs*

¼   *cup plus 2 tablespoons sugar*

1   *teaspoon vanilla extract*

½   *teaspoon grated lemon peel*

12   *Basic Crepes (see recipe, page 179)*

1   *16-ounce bag frozen unsweetened blueberries, thawed*

⅓   *cup sugar*

1   *teaspoon cornstarch*

½   *teaspoon grated lemon peel*

3   *tablespoons (about) unsalted butter*

Powdered sugar
Sour cream (optional)

FOR FILLING: Line large sieve with kitchen towel. Spoon cottage cheese into center. Bring up sides of towel to enclose cottage cheese. Squeeze dry. Transfer 3 cups cheese to processor and blend until smooth. Add eggs, ¼ cup plus 2 tablespoons sugar, vanilla and ½ teaspoon lemon peel and blend well.

Line baking sheet with foil. Divide filling among crepes, mounding in center. Fold 1 side of crepe over filling and press gently to flatten. Fold opposite side over. Fold in remaining 2 sides, enclosing filling and forming packet. Place seam side down on foil-lined sheet. Repeat with remaining crepes.

FOR SAUCE: Combine berries, ⅓ cup sugar, cornstarch and ½ teaspoon lemon peel in heavy large saucepan. Cook over medium heat until reduced to thick sauce, stirring frequently, about 5 minutes. *(Crepes and sauce can be prepared 1 day ahead. Cover crepes and sauce separately and then refrigerate.)*

Preheat oven to 250°F. Melt 1 tablespoon unsalted butter in heavy large skillet over medium heat. Working in batches, place

---

This would make an excellent dessert choice for brunch, after the Leek and Cheese Blintzes with Tomato Coulis on page 100. The Basic Crepes recipe makes enough for both dishes—two courses for the effort of only one.

◆ ◆ ◆

blintzes seam side down in skillet and cook until golden brown and heated through, adding more butter to skillet as necessary and turning once, about 5 minutes. Transfer blintzes to baking sheet; place in oven to keep warm.

Warm sauce until just heated through. Arrange blintzes on platter. Sprinkle with powdered sugar. Top with sour cream if desired. Serve with sauce.

MAKES 12

Basic Crepes

◆ ◆ ◆

2   cups all purpose flour
¼   cup sugar
½   teaspoon salt
6   extra-large eggs
¼   cup (½ stick) unsalted butter, melted, cooled
2   cups (or more) milk

      Additional melted butter

Blend first 3 ingredients in processor. Add eggs and process until blended. Mix in ¼ cup melted butter. Add 2 cups milk and blend until smooth, stopping occasionally to scrape down sides of bowl. Cover and refrigerate batter at least 1 hour or overnight.

If necessary, thin batter to consistency of very heavy cream by adding milk 1 tablespoon at a time. Heat heavy skillet with 7-inch-diameter bottom over medium-high heat. Brush skillet with melted butter. Spoon 3 tablespoons batter into cup; pour into skillet and swirl to coat bottom evenly. Cook until top appears dry, loosening sides of crepe with spatula, about 45 seconds. Turn and cook until brown spots appear on second side, about 30 seconds. Turn out crepe onto plate. Repeat with remaining batter, stacking crepes on plate. *(Can be prepared ahead. Stack crepes between layers of plastic wrap; refrigerate up to 3 days or freeze up to 2 weeks. Thaw frozen crepes before using.)*

MAKES ABOUT 26

Tropical Spa "Sundae"

◆ ◆ ◆

2   very ripe mangoes or papayas, peeled, pitted and coarsely
    chopped
    Maple syrup (optional)

2   cups cubed fresh pineapple
1   cup thinly sliced fresh papaya
1   cup halved strawberries
1   cup sliced banana
2   plums, thinly sliced
    Fresh mint leaves

◆ ◆ ◆

Made with tropical fruits and topped with a luscious mango sauce, this "sundae" is so good you won't miss the ice cream.

◆ ◆ ◆

Puree 2 mangoes or papayas in blender or food processor until smooth. Press through strainer. Sweeten with small amount of maple syrup, if desired.

Divide all remaining fruit among 4 plates, arranging attractively. Drizzle mango or papaya sauce thinly over fruits. Garnish with mint.

4 SERVINGS

The Real Ambrosia

◆ ◆ ◆

²/₃   cup flaked sweetened coconut

6   large oranges
1   pineapple, quartered lengthwise, cored, peeled, sliced
    crosswise
2   tablespoons powdered sugar

Position rack in center of oven and preheat to 375°F. Spread coconut on cookie sheet; bake until golden, stirring occasionally, about 10 minutes. Cool.

Using small sharp knife, cut peel and white pith from oranges. Cut oranges crosswise into ½-inch-thick rounds. Arrange oranges and pineapple on platter. Cover; chill fruit until cold, at least 30 minutes and up to 1½ hours. Sift sugar over. Top with coconut.

8 SERVINGS

Plum-Peach Crisp

◆ ◆ ◆

1   cup all purpose flour
½   cup packed dark brown sugar
½   cup (1 stick) chilled unsalted butter, cut into pieces
2   teaspoons minced orange peel (orange part only)
¼   teaspoon salt

2¾ pounds plums, pitted, cut into ½-inch wedges
4   medium peaches, peeled, pitted, cut into ½-inch wedges
½   cup sugar
2   tablespoons quick-cooking tapioca
1   teaspoon fresh lemon juice
    Pinch of salt

    Vanilla ice cream or frozen yogurt

FOR TOPPING: Combine first 5 ingredients in processor. Using on/off turns, process until mixture forms small moist clumps. *(Can be prepared 1 day ahead. Cover and refrigerate.)*

FOR FILLING: Mix plums and next 5 ingredients in bowl. Let stand at least 30 minutes. and up to 2 hours, stirring occasionally.

Position rack in center of oven and preheat to 350°F. Butter 8 x 8 x 2-inch glass baking dish. Spoon filling into prepared dish. Sprinkle topping over. Bake until fruit is tender and topping is brown and crisp, about 45 minutes.

Spoon warm crisp into deep bowls. Place scoop of ice cream or frozen yogurt atop and serve.

6 SERVINGS

◆ ◆ ◆

DRINKS AND DESSERT FOR A CROWD

◆ ◆ ◆

Mexican Chocolate and Almond Cake

◆ ◆ ◆

1²⁄₃ *cups sliced almonds, toasted (about 6 ounces)*
4½ *ounces semisweet chocolate, chopped*
2½ *teaspoons grated orange peel*
1 *teaspoon ground cinnamon*
5 *eggs, separated*
6 *tablespoons sugar*

4 *ounces semisweet chocolate, chopped*
½ *cup half and half*
¼ *teaspoon ground cinnamon*

½ *cup chilled whipping cream*
1½ *tablespoons sugar*
 Ground cinnamon
3 *oranges, peel and white pith removed, sliced into rounds*

FOR CAKE: Preheat oven to 350°F. Line bottom of 8-inch square baking pan with parchment. Finely grind almonds, 4½ ounces chocolate, orange peel and 1 teaspoon cinnamon in processor. In medium bowl of electric mixer, beat yolks and 3 tablespoons sugar until light yellow and slightly thickened, about 3 minutes. Mix in nut mixture (mixture will be very thick). Using clean dry bowl and beaters, beat egg whites until soft peaks form. Add 3 tablespoons sugar and beat until stiff but not dry. Mix half of whites into chocolate mixture to lighten. Gently fold in remaining whites.

Transfer batter to prepared pan. Bake until tester inserted into center comes out clean, about 35 minutes. Cool in pan on rack. Turn out cake and remove paper. *(Can be made 1 day ahead. Wrap tightly; store at room temperature.)*

FOR SAUCE: Melt 4 ounces chocolate in heavy small saucepan over low heat, stirring until smooth. Mix in half and half and ¼ teaspoon cinnamon and stir until smooth. Cool.

Whip cream and 1½ tablespoons sugar until peaks form. Cut cake into squares. Top each with whipped cream. Sprinkle with cinnamon and drizzle with chocolate sauce. Garnish with orange slices.

6 SERVINGS

◆ ◆ ◆

This would be a fitting finale to a Mexican-style meal. Leftover cake is great for breakfast or a snack.

◆ ◆ ◆

Chocolate-Sour Cream Layer Cake

◆ ◆ ◆

1   cup sifted all purpose flour
6   tablespoons unsweetened cocoa powder
$^1/_2$ teaspoon salt
$^1/_4$ teaspoon baking powder
$^1/_4$ teaspoon baking soda
10   tablespoons ($1^1/_4$ sticks) unsalted butter, room temperature
1   cup plus 2 tablespoons sugar
1   teaspoon vanilla extract
2   large eggs
$^1/_2$ cup sour cream, room temperature

2   teaspoons instant coffee powder
$1^1/_2$ teaspoons hot water
1   cup plus 2 tablespoons sour cream
10   ounces semisweet chocolate, chopped

     Chocolate curls (optional)

FOR CAKE: Position rack in lowest third of oven and preheat to 350°F. Grease two 8-inch-diameter cake pans with 2-inch-high sides. Line bottoms with parchment; grease parchment. Sift first 5 ingredients into small bowl. Using electric mixer, beat butter in large bowl until fluffy. Gradually beat in sugar. Beat in vanilla extract. Add eggs 1 at a time, beating well after each addition. Add dry ingredients alternately with $^1/_2$ cup sour cream in 2 additions each, beating just until blended.

Divide batter between prepared cake pans; smooth top. Bake until cakes begin to shrink from sides of pans, about 25 minutes. Cool cakes in pans on racks 5 minutes. Turn out cakes onto racks; peel off parchment. Turn cakes right side up onto racks and cool.

FOR FROSTING: Dissolve coffee powder in hot water in bowl. Add 1 cup plus 2 tablespoons sour cream and whisk to blend. Melt chocolate in top of double boiler over simmering water, stirring until smooth. Add sour cream mixture to chocolate; whisk to blend. Remove mixture from over water.

Place 1 cake layer flat side up on platter. Immediately spread $^1/_2$ cup frosting over. Top with second cake layer, flat side up. Spread top and sides with remaining frosting. (If frosting becomes too stiff, place over warm water and stir until slightly softened.) Garnish cake with chocolate curls, if desired. *(Can be prepared 8 hours ahead. Cover and let stand at room temperature.)*

10 SERVINGS

◆ ◆ ◆

This old-fashioned chocolate cake, with its classic chocolate-sour cream frosting, might define the word *Americana* from a dessert perspective.

Strawberry Cheesecake in Macaroon Crust

◆ ◆ ◆

3   *1-pint baskets strawberries, hulled, halved*

$\frac{1}{2}$ *cup sugar*

2   *tablespoons fresh lemon juice*

$\frac{1}{4}$ *cup packed dried apricots (about 1$\frac{1}{2}$ ounces)*

$\frac{1}{4}$ *cup water*

$\frac{1}{3}$ *cup sugar*

2   *large egg whites*

$2\frac{1}{4}$ *cups shredded unsweetened coconut,* toasted (about 5 ounces)*

$1\frac{1}{2}$ *pounds cream cheese, room temperature*

$1\frac{1}{4}$ *cups sugar*

$\frac{1}{4}$ *teaspoon salt*

$\frac{3}{4}$ *cup sour cream*

1   *tablespoon dark rum*

1   *tablespoon fresh lemon juice*

2   *teaspoons vanilla extract*

3   *large eggs*

$1\frac{1}{2}$ *1-pint baskets strawberries, hulled, halved lengthwise, stems intact*
      Fresh mint sprigs (optional)

FOR SAUCE: Bring first 3 ingredients to boil in heavy large saucepan over high heat. Reduce heat to medium-low and simmer until mixture has thick syrup consistency, stirring occasionally, about 1 hour. Cool. *(Can be prepared 2 days ahead. Cover and refrigerate.)*

FOR CRUST: Bring apricots and water to boil in heavy small saucepan. Cover, remove from heat and let stand until fruit is soft, about 30 minutes.

Drain apricots and pat dry. Place in processor. Add $\frac{1}{3}$ cup sugar and egg whites and process until mixture has thick fluffy consistency and apricots are minced, scraping down sides of work bowl occasionally. Add $\frac{1}{2}$ cup coconut and process until minced. Transfer mixture to medium bowl. Stir in remaining coconut. Freeze until firm, about 20 minutes.

Position rack in center of oven and preheat to 350°F. Wrap heavy-duty foil around outside of 9-inch springform pan with $2\frac{3}{4}$-inch-high sides. Spoon coconut mixture into prepared pan. Wrap plastic wrap around fingertips and press coconut mixture

evenly over bottom and 2 inches up sides of pan to form crust. Bake crust until light brown, about 15 minutes. Remove from oven. Maintain oven temperature.

FOR FILLING: Using electric mixer, beat cream cheese, $1\frac{1}{4}$ cups sugar and salt in large bowl until smooth. Add sour cream, rum, 1 tablespoon lemon juice and vanilla and beat until well blended. Add eggs and beat just until blended. Transfer to crust.

Bake cheesecake until brown, puffed and firm in center, about 1 hour. Cool cake in pan on rack 10 minutes. Cut around pan sides to loosen crust. Cool. Cover and refrigerate overnight.

Cut around pan sides to loosen cake. Release pan sides. Arrange berry halves over top of cake. Garnish with mint, if desired. Serve with strawberry sauce.

*Available in natural foods stores and some supermarkets.

10 TO 12 SERVINGS

Chocolate Soufflé Cake with Banana Cream

1/3   cup whipping cream

2/3   cup milk (do not use low-fat or nonfat)

1/3   cup sugar

4   large egg yolks

9   ounces bittersweet (not unsweetened) or semisweet
     chocolate, chopped

3/4   cup (1 1/2 sticks) unsalted butter, room temperature

1   cup sugar

3   large eggs

1   teaspoon vanilla extract

1   cup all purpose flour

1 1/2 teaspoons baking powder

1/4   teaspoon salt

4   medium bananas, peeled
2   tablespoons sugar
2   tablespoons dark rum
2   cups chilled whipping cream

    Powdered sugar

FOR CAKE: Bring ⅓ cup cream, ⅓ cup milk and ⅓ cup sugar to simmer in heavy medium saucepan over medium-high heat, stirring until sugar dissolves. Whisk yolks to blend in bowl. Gradually whisk in hot cream mixture. Return mixture to same saucepan. Stir over medium-low heat until custard thickens and leaves path on back of spoon when finger is drawn across, 3 minutes; do not boil. Add chocolate; whisk until melted. Cool to room temperature.

Preheat oven to 350°F. Lightly butter and flour 9-inch-diameter springform pan with 2½-inch-high sides. Line bottom of pan with parchment. Butter and flour parchment lightly. Wrap outside of springform pan completely with 2 layers of heavy-duty foil.

Using electric mixer, beat butter and 1 cup sugar in medium bowl 6 minutes, scraping sides of bowl as necessary. Add eggs 1 at a time, beating well after each addition. Add vanilla and beat until very light and fluffy, about 6 minutes. Add butter mixture to chocolate mixture and fold until well incorporated. Sift flour, baking powder and salt into medium bowl. Fold flour mixture into chocolate mixture alternately with ⅓ cup milk in 3 additions, beginning and ending with flour mixture.

Pour batter into prepared pan. Place springform pan in roasting pan. Pour water into roasting pan to depth of 1¼ inches. Bake cake 45 minutes. Cover top of cake loosely with foil. Continue to bake until top of cake forms hard crust, is firm to touch and tester inserted into center comes out with moist batter still attached, about 1 hour more. Cool to room temperature. Cake may crack and fall as it cools. Cover and chill overnight. *(Can be made 2 days ahead.)*

FOR BANANA CREAM: Preheat oven to 350°F. Place bananas in baking dish. Roast 15 minutes. Cool completely. Place bananas, 2 tablespoons sugar and rum in processor; puree. Add 2 cups cream and process until fluffy, about 2 minutes. *(Can be made 4 hours ahead. Cover and refrigerate.)*

Preheat oven to 325°F. Cut cold cake into wedges. Place each wedge on ovenproof plate. Warm in oven until heated through, about 7 minutes. Dust each lightly with powdered sugar. Pass banana cream separately.

8 SERVINGS

Strawberry and Chocolate Nut Cake

◆ ◆ ◆

Butter
Unsweetened cocoa
1¼ *cups sugar*
½ *cup whole almonds, toasted, cooled*
½ *cup walnuts, toasted, cooled*
1 *cup mini chocolate chips (about 6 ounces)*
⅓ *cup all purpose flour*

6 *large eggs, separated, room temperature*
1 *tablespoon minced orange peel (orange part only)*
¼ *teaspoon salt*

4 *large egg yolks*
½ *cup sugar*
¼ *cup all purpose flour*
1 *vanilla bean, split lengthwise*
2 *cups half and half*

3 *tablespoons water*
1 *envelope unflavored gelatin*

1 *cup chilled whipping cream*
⅓ *cup sugar*

2 *cups thinly sliced hulled strawberries (about 1½ 1-pint baskets)*

4 *ounces bittersweet (not unsweetened) or semisweet chocolate, shaved or grated*
8 *large strawberries*

FOR CAKE: Position rack in center of oven and preheat to 350°F. Lightly butter two 9-inch-diameter cake pans with 1½-inch-high sides. Line bottom of pans with waxed paper. Butter paper. Dust with cocoa. Finely grind ¼ cup sugar and nuts in processor. Transfer to medium bowl. Mix in chocolate chips and ⅓ cup flour.

Using electric mixer, beat yolks and ½ cup sugar in large bowl until very thick and pale, about 4 minutes. Mix in orange peel, then nut mixture. Using clean dry beaters, beat egg whites and salt in another large bowl until soft peaks form. Gradually add ½ cup sugar and beat until stiff but not dry. Fold whites into chocolate mixture in 2 additions. Divide between prepared pans.

Bake cakes until tester inserted into center comes out clean, about 35 minutes. Cool cakes in pans on racks 30 minutes. Turn out onto racks. Peel off paper; cool completely. *(Can be prepared up to 1 day ahead. Return cakes to pans; cover tightly. Let cakes stand at room temperature.)*

FOR FROSTING: Whisk yolks, ½ cup sugar and ¼ cup flour in medium bowl until blended. Scrape seeds from vanilla bean into heavy medium saucepan; add bean and half and half. Bring to simmer over medium-high heat. Gradually add half and half mixture to yolk mixture, whisking until smooth. Return mixture to same saucepan and whisk over medium-high heat until pastry cream thickens and boils, about 5 minutes. Strain into bowl.

Place 3 tablespoons water in heavy small saucepan. Sprinkle gelatin over; let stand 10 minutes to soften. Stir over low heat until gelatin dissolves. Whisk into hot pastry cream. Set mixture over bowl of ice water. Let pastry cream stand until cold but not set, whisking often, about 30 minutes.

Beat whipping cream and ⅓ cup sugar in bowl until firm peaks form. Fold into pastry cream. Chill until just beginning to set, approximately 30 minutes.

Place 1 cake layer on platter. Spread 1 cup frosting over. Arrange sliced strawberries in concentric circles over frosting, overlapping tightly. Place second cake layer over, pressing gently. Spread remaining frosting over entire cake. Chill until frosting sets, approximately 30 minutes.

Press chocolate shavings onto sides of cake. Slice berries thinly from point to stem, leaving stems intact. Press berries gently to fan. Arrange around top edge of cake. *(Can be made 8 hours ahead. Chill.)*

10 TO 12 SERVINGS

◆ ◆ ◆

Delicate chocolate-studded nut cake, rich vanilla pastry cream and sliced strawberries come together for an impressive dessert.

◆ ◆ ◆

Chocolate Hazelnut Cake

◆ ◆ ◆

1/2   cup whipping cream

1   tablespoon light corn syrup

8   ounces imported milk chocolate (such as Lindt), chopped

1/2   cup hazelnuts, toasted, husked

2   teaspoons powdered sugar

1   cup sifted all purpose flour

1/3   cup unsweetened cocoa powder

1/2   teaspoon salt

1/4   teaspoon baking powder

1/4   teaspoon baking soda

1 1/2   tablespoons hot water

1   tablespoon instant espresso powder or instant coffee powder

1/2   cup buttermilk

3/4   cup (1 1/2 sticks) unsalted butter, room temperature

1 1/3   cups sugar

1   teaspoon vanilla extract

3   large eggs

6   ounces bittersweet (not unsweetened) or semisweet chocolate, chopped

1/2   cup (1 stick) unsalted butter, cut into pieces

1   tablespoon light corn syrup

12   whole hazelnuts, husked

FOR FILLING: Bring cream and 1 tablespoon corn syrup to simmer in heavy small saucepan. Place milk chocolate in medium bowl. Pour hot cream mixture over and let stand 1 minute. Stir until chocolate melts and mixture is smooth. Set aside.

Blend 1/2 cup hazelnuts and powdered sugar in processor until paste forms, stopping to scrape down sides. Stir paste into chocolate mixture. Chill until cool but still spreadable, about 2 hours.

FOR CAKE: Position rack in lowest third of oven and preheat to 350°F. Butter 9-inch-diameter cake pan with 2-inch-high sides. Line bottom with parchment. Dust pan with flour; tap out excess. Sift flour and next 4 ingredients into medium bowl. Stir hot water and espresso powder in small bowl until espresso dissolves. Mix in buttermilk. Using electric mixer, beat 3/4 cup butter in large bowl until light and fluffy. Gradually beat in sugar and vanilla. Add eggs 1 at a time, beating well after each addition. Beat in dry ingredients alternately with buttermilk mixture in 2 additions.

Pour batter into prepared pan. Bake until tester inserted into center comes out clean, about 45 minutes. Cool cake in pan on rack 5 minutes. Turn out cake onto rack. Peel off parchment. Turn right side up onto another rack and cool.

Using wooden spoon, beat filling until slightly softened and lightened in color, about 30 seconds. Cut cake horizontally in half. Place 1 layer cut side up on platter. Slide waxed paper strips under edges of cake. Spread half of filling over cake. Top with second layer, cut side down. Spread remaining filling over top and sides of cake. Chill 10 minutes.

MEANWHILE, PREPARE GLAZE: Combine bittersweet chocolate, ½ cup butter and 1 tablespoon syrup in top of double boiler over simmering water. Stir until smooth. Remove from over water. Cool to lukewarm, stirring occasionally.

Pour glaze in pool over center of cake. Using icing spatula, spread over top and sides of cake. Arrange 12 nuts around top edge.

12 SERVINGS

Flourless Chocolate Torte

◆ ◆ ◆

7   ounces bittersweet (not unsweetened) or semisweet
     chocolate, chopped
¾   cup (1½ sticks) unsalted butter
4   large eggs
1⅓ cups sugar
1   teaspoon instant espresso powder or instant coffee powder

Preheat oven to 325°F. Butter and sugar 8-inch-diameter springform pan. Wrap foil around outside of pan. Melt chocolate and butter in heavy medium saucepan over low heat, stirring until smooth. Whisk eggs, sugar and espresso powder in large bowl until well blended. Whisk in chocolate mixture.

Pour batter into prepared pan. Place cake in large baking pan. Add enough hot water to baking pan to come halfway up sides of cake. Bake until knife inserted into center comes out clean, about 1½ hours (cake will be about ½ inch high). Remove cake from water bath. Cool. Remove foil. Cover and refrigerate over-night. *(Can be prepared 1 week ahead; keep refrigerated.)* Release pan sides from cake. Cut cake into wedges. Serve cold.

12 SERVINGS

Classic Tiramisù

◆ ◆ ◆

2   cups Marsala
1½ cups sugar
12 egg yolks

½   cup hot water
2   teaspoons instant espresso powder or instant coffee powder
1   pound mascarpone cheese*

3   3-ounce packages soft ladyfingers, split in half
2   tablespoons unsweetened cocoa powder

Whisk 1½ cups Marsala, ¾ cup sugar and yolks in large metal bowl. Set bowl over saucepan of simmering water. Using portable electric mixer, beat mixture until candy thermometer registers 160°F, about 15 minutes. Remove bowl from over hot water. Set zabaglione aside.

Combine hot water and instant espresso powder in large bowl; stir to dissolve. Add mascarpone cheese and remaining ¾ cup sugar and beat to blend.

Cover bottom of 9 x 13 x 2-inch glass baking dish with single layer of ladyfingers, flat side up. Brush ¼ cup Marsala over. Spread 2 cups mascarpone mixture over ladyfingers. Top with 2½ cups zabaglione. Arrange another layer of ladyfingers over zabaglione, flat side up. Brush with ¼ cup Marsala. Spread remaining mascarpone mixture over. Cover with remaining zabaglione. Sift cocoa over. Cover and chill at least 6 hours. *(Can be made 1 day ahead.)*

Cut tiramisù into squares and transfer to plates (if tiramisù is soft, spoon onto plates). Serve immediately.

*Italian cream cheese available at Italian markets and some specialty foods stores. If unavailable, blend 1 pound cream cheese with 6 tablespoons whipping cream and ¼ cup sour cream. Use 2 cups (packed) mixture for recipe.

8 SERVINGS

Two versions of one of the most popular desserts of the year — tiramisù. The traditional Italian one combines a Marsala-spiked zabaglione custard, mascarpone cheese and lady fingers. A fresh interpretation of the classic uses berries and fruit liqueur (fresh berries as a garnish, frozen berries in the filling to keep it moist).

◆ ◆ ◆

Mixed Berry Tiramisù

◆ ◆ ◆

1   *12-ounce package unsweetened frozen mixed berries*
12   *tablespoons sugar*

1   *10-ounce package frozen raspberries in syrup, thawed*
¼   *cup raspberry liqueur*
3   *4.4-ounce packages Champagne biscuits (4-inch-long*
      ladyfinger-like biscuits)

3   *8-ounce containers mascarpone cheese**
2   *teaspoons vanilla extract*
1   *1-pint basket strawberries, hulled*
2   *½-pint baskets raspberries*
1   *½-pint basket blueberries*

Cook frozen mixed berries and 6 tablespoons sugar in heavy medium saucepan over medium heat until mixture resembles jam and is reduced to 1 cup, stirring frequently, about 15 minutes. Cool.

Strain syrup from thawed raspberries through sieve set over bowl, pressing gently on solids. Discard solids. Add raspberry liqueur to raspberry syrup in bowl. Using sharp knife, trim 1 biscuit to 3-inch (about) length. Quickly dip biscuit into syrup, turning to coat lightly. Place rounded end up and sugared side against side of 9-inch-diameter springform pan with 2¾-inch-high sides. Repeat with as many biscuits as necessary to cover sides of pan. Dip more biscuits in syrup and arrange on bottom of pan, covering completely.

In bowl, whisk mascarpone with 6 tablespoons sugar and vanilla to blend. Set aside. Thinly slice enough strawberries to measure ½ cup. Gently spread half of jam mixture over biscuits in bottom of pan. Spoon half of mascarpone mixture over; smooth top. Sprinkle with sliced strawberries, ½ cup fresh raspberries and ½ cup blueberries. Dip more biscuits into syrup; arrange over fruit in pan, covering completely and trimming to fit. Gently spread remaining jam mixture over biscuits. Spoon remaining mascarpone mixture over; smooth top. Cover; chill at least 4 hours or overnight.

Release pan sides. Transfer cake to platter. Arrange remaining fresh berries decoratively atop cake and serve.

*Italian cream cheese available at Italian markets and some specialty foods stores. If unavailable, blend 1½ pounds cream cheese with ½ cup whipping cream and 6 tablespoons sour cream. Use 3 cups mixture for recipe.

10 SERVINGS

Chilled Essencia Sabayon with Pineapple and Oranges

❖ ❖ ❖

4   *large egg yolks*
¼   *cup plus 1 tablespoon sugar*
½   *cup plus 3 tablespoons Essencia or other sweet dessert wine*

⅓   *cup chilled whipping cream*

3   *oranges*
½   *large pineapple, peeled, cored, cut into 1-inch pieces*

   Fresh mint sprigs

Whisk yolks and ¼ cup sugar in small metal bowl. Gradually whisk in ½ cup Essencia. Set bowl over saucepan of simmering water and whisk until candy thermometer registers 160°F, about 10 minutes. Cover and chill until cold, whisking occasionally.

Using electric mixer, whip cream in medium bowl to soft peaks. Fold cream into sabayon. *(Can be prepared 6 hours ahead. Chill.)*

Using small sharp knife, cut off peel and white pith from oranges. Working over bowl to catch juices, cut between membranes to release segments. Add pineapple. Mix fruit with remaining 1 tablespoon sugar and 3 tablespoons Essencia. Divide fruit among 4 bowls. Top each with dollop of sabayon. Garnish with mint and serve.

4 SERVINGS

Essencia is a lovely dessert wine made by the Quady Winery in Central California. Many fine wine shops and liquor stores stock it. A touch of whipped cream gives this delicate topping a mousselike texture. Vary the fruit by season, using berries and peaches in the summer months.

Vanilla Flan

❖ ❖ ❖

1¼ *cups sugar*
⅓   *cup water*

2   *cups half and half*
1   *cup whipping cream*
½   *cup plus 2 tablespoons sweetened condensed milk*
3   *large eggs*
2   *large egg yolks*
1   *tablespoon vanilla extract*

Preheat oven to 300°F. Stir sugar and water in heavy medium saucepan over low heat until sugar dissolves. Increase heat and boil without stirring until syrup turns deep brown, brushing down sides of pan with pastry brush dipped into water and swirling pan occasionally. Pour caramel evenly into eight $^3/_4$-cup custard cups. Set aside.

Bring half and half, cream and condensed milk to simmer in heavy medium saucepan. Whisk eggs and yolks in medium bowl to blend. Gradually whisk hot half and half mixture into yolk mixture. Whisk in vanilla.

Ladle custard into caramel-lined cups. Place cups in large baking pan. Add enough hot water to pan to come halfway up sides of cups. Bake until custards no longer move in center when cups are gently shaken, about 40 minutes. Remove custards from water and cool 1 hour. Cover and chill overnight.

Run small sharp knife around custards to loosen if necessary. Turn out onto plates and serve.

8 SERVINGS

Hot Lemon-Lime Soufflé

◆ ◆ ◆

Sugar
2   *cups milk*
1   *cup plus 3 tablespoons powdered sugar*
7   *large egg yolks*
$^1/_3$ *cup all purpose flour*
6   *tablespoons fresh lemon juice*
2   *tablespoons fresh lime juice*
5   *teaspoons grated lime peel*

6   *large egg whites*
$^1/_4$ *cup sugar*

Preheat oven to 350°F. Butter 10-cup soufflé dish; sprinkle with sugar. Bring 2 cups milk to boil in heavy medium saucepan. Whisk powdered sugar, 4 egg yolks and flour in medium bowl to blend. Gradually pour hot milk into egg mixture, whisking constantly. Return mixture to same saucepan. Cook over medium-high heat until mixture thickens and boils, stirring constantly, about 3 minutes. Transfer soufflé base to bowl and cool slightly. Stir in fresh lemon juice, lime juice, lime peel and remaining 3 egg yolks.

In large bowl, beat egg whites to soft peaks. Gradually add $^1/_4$ cup sugar and beat until stiff peaks form. Fold egg whites into soufflé base in 2 additions. Pour into prepared dish. Bake until soufflé is puffed and top is golden, about 50 minutes. Serve immediately.

2 SERVINGS

Fools are light desserts made of fruit and whipped cream. They date back to fifteenth-century England. White chocolate gives this classic a contemporary twist.

◆ ◆ ◆

Lime Fool with Strawberries and Kiwi

◆ ◆ ◆

$^1/_4$ cup whipping cream

$^1/_4$ cup fresh lime juice

1 teaspoon grated lime peel

6 ounces imported white chocolate (such as Lindt), chopped

$^3/_4$ cup chilled whipping cream

3 tablespoons sugar

2 cups sliced hulled strawberries

2 kiwi fruit, peeled, thinly sliced

4 whole strawberries

4 lime slices

Bring first 3 ingredients to simmer in heavy small saucepan. Reduce heat to low. Add chocolate and stir until melted and smooth. Pour into medium bowl. Refrigerate until cool but not set, stirring occasionally, about 25 minutes.

Beat $^3/_4$ cup chilled whipping cream in another medium bowl to soft peaks. Add sugar and beat until stiff peaks form. Fold cream into white chocolate mixture.

Place scant $^1/_4$ cup sliced berries in each of four 8- to 10-ounce wineglasses. Press 3 kiwi slices against sides of each glass. Spoon $^1/_3$ cup cream mixture into each glass. Spoon scant $^1/_4$ cup sliced berries in center of each, pressing into center so berries do not show at sides of glasses. Spoon remaining cream over; smooth tops. Cover and chill at least 2 and up to 6 hours.

To serve, using small knife, make lengthwise cuts in whole strawberries without cutting through stem ends. Fan 1 strawberry atop each dessert. Attach lime slice to rim of each glass.

4 SERVINGS

Raspberry-filled Chocolate Mousse

◆ ◆ ◆

9   ounces semisweet chocolate, chopped
1   ounce unsweetened chocolate, chopped

½   cup sugar
3   tablespoons water
3   tablespoons light corn syrup

3   large egg whites
½   teaspoon cream of tartar

2½ cups chilled whipping cream
2   teaspoons vanilla extract

2   ½-pint baskets fresh raspberries

1   tablespoon powdered sugar

Combine semisweet chocolate and unsweetened chocolate in large metal bowl. Set over saucepan of simmering water and stir until melted. Remove bowl from over water. Cool to lukewarm.

Combine ½ cup sugar, water and corn syrup in heavy small saucepan. Stir over medium heat until sugar dissolves. Increase heat to high and boil until syrup registers 238°F on candy thermometer, approximately 5 minutes.

Meanwhile, using electric mixer, beat egg whites and cream of tartar in large bowl until soft peaks form.

Gradually add boiling syrup to egg whites, beating until meringue is stiff and cool, about 5 minutes. Whisk ⅓ of egg whites into lukewarm chocolate to lighten. Fold remaining whites into chocolate. In large bowl, beat 1½ cups cream and 1 teaspoon vanilla to soft peaks. Fold into chocolate mixture.

Set aside ½ cup raspberries for garnish. Divide half of chocolate mixture among 8 large stemmed glasses. Sprinkle remaining raspberries over mousse, placing some berries against sides of each glass. Spoon remaining chocolate mousse over raspberries, dividing evenly. Refrigerate at least 3 hours or overnight.

Beat remaining 1 cup whipping cream, 1 teaspoon vanilla and powdered sugar to soft peaks. Spoon whipped cream mixture over mousse in each glass. Scatter reserved raspberries over.

8 SERVINGS

Bittersweet Chocolate Soufflés

◆ ◆ ◆

7   ounces bittersweet (not unsweetened) chocolate, chopped
7   tablespoons unsalted butter

6   large egg yolks
7   tablespoons sugar

5   large egg whites, room temperature
4   ounces bittersweet (not unsweetened) chocolate, cut into 8 pieces

Preheat oven to 350°F. Butter eight ³⁄₄-cup custard cups or soufflé dishes. Stir 7 ounces chocolate and butter in heavy medium saucepan over low heat until melted. Pour into large bowl and cool.

Using electric mixer, beat yolks and sugar in medium bowl until pale yellow and slowly dissolving ribbon forms when beaters are lifted. Fold yolk mixture into chocolate mixture.

Using electric mixer fitted with clean dry beaters, beat whites in another medium bowl to soft peaks. Fold ¹⁄₃ of whites into chocolate mixture to lighten, then fold in remaining whites. Spoon soufflé mixture into prepared custard cups, filling each ²⁄₃ full. Place 1 piece of chocolate in center of each. Cover with remaining soufflé mixture. *(Can be prepared up to 45 minutes ahead. Let soufflés stand at room temperature.)*

Bake until soufflés rise but center of each still moves when cups are gently shaken, about 15 minutes. Transfer to plates.

MAKES 8

Sticky Toffee Pudding

◆ ◆ ◆

³⁄₄   cup sugar
¹⁄₄   cup (¹⁄₂ stick) unsalted butter, room temperature
1   large egg
1¹⁄₂ cups all purpose flour
1   teaspoon baking powder
1¹⁄₄ cups boiling water
1   cup chopped pitted dates
2   teaspoons instant espresso powder or instant coffee powder

1 teaspoon vanilla extract
1 teaspoon baking soda

$^1/_3$ cup firmly packed brown sugar
3 tablespoons unsalted butter
2 tablespoons whipping cream

FOR PUDDING: Preheat oven to 350°F. Butter six $^3/_4$-cup custard cups. Using electric mixer, beat sugar and $^1/_4$ cup butter in large bowl until combined. Add egg and beat 2 minutes. Sift in flour and baking powder and beat 1 minute. Mix boiling water, dates, espresso powder, vanilla and baking soda in metal bowl. Add to butter mixture; beat until well blended. Divide batter among prepared custard cups. Bake until golden brown and tester inserted into centers comes out clean, 30 minutes. Transfer to rack; cool 10 minutes.

MEANWHILE, PREPARE SAUCE: Bring brown sugar and next 2 ingredients to simmer in heavy small saucepan, stirring to dissolve sugar. Simmer 3 minutes, stirring occasionally.

Preheat broiler. Pour sauce over warm puddings. Broil until slightly caramelized, 2 minutes. Serve immediately.

MAKES 6

Rice Pudding with Dried Cherries

◆ ◆ ◆

$3\,^1/_3$ cups (or more) milk
$^2/_3$ cup short-grain or medium-grain rice
$^1/_2$ cup dried tart cherries, dried cranberries or dried Bing cherries
$^1/_3$ cup sugar
$^1/_2$ vanilla bean, split lengthwise
$^1/_4$ teaspoon (generous) salt
$^1/_4$ cup pure maple syrup
$2\,^1/_2$ tablespoons bourbon (optional)

Combine $3^1/_3$ cups milk, rice, cherries, sugar, vanilla bean and salt in heavy medium saucepan. Bring to boil, stirring occasionally. Reduce heat to low and cook uncovered until rice is tender and mixture is thick, stirring frequently, about 35 minutes. Mix in maple syrup and bourbon, if desired. Serve pudding hot, at room temperature or chilled, thinning with more milk if too thick.

6 SERVINGS

CHERRIES FROM MICHIGAN

Michigan is cherry country, with about 75 percent of the nation's total coming from the state's 970 growers and their four million trees. The bulk of that total is harvested in the five counties around Traverse City, the Cherry Capital of the World.

Michigan grows two different kinds of cherries, the sweet type, which is mostly eaten fresh or prepared for maraschino cherries, and the tart Montmorency cherry, a ruby-red variety that is used for cooking, baking, preserving and drying. (The dried are the most widely available form of Michigan cherry stocked in supermarkets across the country.)

◆ ◆ ◆

A CELEBRATION OF
STRAWBERRIES

Gingered Grapefruit Baskets

♦ ♦ ♦

6   *pink grapefruits*

Vanilla ice cream or frozen yogurt
¹/₃   cup firmly packed golden brown sugar
4 ¹/₂ teaspoons finely chopped peeled fresh ginger

Fresh mint leaves

Cut grapefruits horizontally in half. Using grapefruit knife or paring knife, cut all around grapefruit halves and between membranes to release segments. Place segments in bowl, discarding seeds. Cut all membranes from 6 grapefruit halves; discard remaining grapefruit halves.

Place large scoop of ice cream in each reserved grapefruit half. Cover and place in freezer until ready to use. Add sugar and ginger to grapefruit in bowl and toss gently. Cover and refrigerate at least 2 hours or overnight.

Spoon some grapefruit mixture over ice cream in each grapefruit basket. Garnish with mint. Serve, passing remaining grapefruit mixture separately.

MAKES 6

♦ ♦ ♦

A pretty dessert that can be made one day ahead, leaving just a quick assembly before serving.

♦ ♦ ♦

Ice Cream Sundaes in Cinnamon Cookie Cups

◆ ◆ ◆

10 ounces bittersweet (not unsweetened) chocolate, chopped
½ cup (or more) milk
½ teaspoon vanilla extract

2 teaspoons fresh lime juice
5 tablespoons unsalted butter
3 tablespoons sugar
2 tablespoons light corn syrup
1 tablespoon all purpose flour
½ teaspoon ground cinnamon
1½ teaspoon grated lime peel
½ cup finely chopped almonds

Vanilla ice cream

FOR SAUCE: Combine chocolate and ½ cup milk in top of double boiler over simmering water. Stir until chocolate melts. Remove from over water. Add vanilla. *(Can be made 1 day ahead. Chill.)*

FOR COOKIES: Position rack in center of oven and preheat to 350°F. Line heavy large cookie sheet with foil. Invert 2 custard cups on work surface. Cover each with paper towel, tucking under cup to secure. Boil lime juice in heavy small saucepan until reduced to glaze, about 1 minute. Reduce heat to low. Add butter, sugar, corn syrup, flour, cinnamon and ½ teaspoon lime peel; stir until butter melts. Remove from heat; mix in nuts.

Drop 1 tablespoon batter in center of upper half of prepared cookie sheet. Drop another tablespoon batter on lower half of same sheet. Bake until mixture spreads, bubbles and turns deep caramel color, about 10 minutes. Cool cookies on sheet just until beginning to firm, about 45 seconds. Run small sharp knife around cookie edges to loosen. Using metal spatula, lift cookie off sheet and drape over 1 inverted custard cup. Repeat with second cookie, returning briefly to oven if cookie has begun to harden. Remove cookie cups from custard cups. Repeat with remaining batter in batches.

Cool cookie cups completely. Immediately transfer to airtight container (cookies will be very fragile). *(Can be made 1 day ahead.)*

Heat sauce in double boiler, stirring occasionally and thinning with more milk if too thick. Place 1 cookie cup on each of 6 plates. Fill each with scoop of ice cream. Drizzle sauce over. Top with lime peel.

6 SERVINGS

Strawberry Daiquiri Sorbet

♦ ♦ ♦

1½ cups water
1 cup sugar

4 1-pint baskets strawberries, hulled
¼ cup dark rum
2 tablespoons fresh lime juice
2 tablespoons triple sec or other orange liqueur

Additional dark rum (optional)

Stir water and sugar in heavy medium saucepan over high heat until sugar dissolves and syrup comes to boil. Remove sugar syrup from heat and then cool.

Puree strawberries in processor or blender. Strain into medium bowl. Mix ¼ cup rum, lime juice, triple sec and sugar syrup into puree. Refrigerate until cold.

Process mixture in ice cream maker according to manufacturer's instructions. Transfer to container; cover tightly. Freeze until firm, about 1 hour. *(Can be prepared 2 days ahead. Keep frozen.)*

Scoop sorbet into bowls. Splash with additional rum, if desired.

MAKES 6 CUPS

Frozen Milky Way Mousse with Bittersweet Chocolate Sauce

♦ ♦ ♦

1 cup whipping cream
½ cup sugar
⅓ cup unsweetened cocoa powder
3 tablespoons unsalted butter
1 teaspoon vanilla extract
½ teaspoon instant coffee powder

1½ cups ½-inch pieces Milky Way bars (about 8¼ ounces)
6 ounces semisweet chocolate, chopped
3 ounces unsweetened chocolate, chopped
4 tablespoons (½ stick) unsalted butter

½ cup sugar
3 tablespoons water

3   large egg whites
¼   teaspoon cream of tartar

1¼ cups chilled whipping cream
1   teaspoon vanilla extract

FOR SAUCE: Combine 1 cup whipping cream, ½ cup sugar, unsweetened cocoa powder and 3 tablespoons unsalted butter in heavy medium saucepan. Bring to simmer over medium-low heat, whisking constantly until butter melts and sugar and cocoa dissolve. Remove from heat and whisk in 1 teaspoon vanilla extract and instant coffee powder. Cool sauce. *(Can be prepared 1 week ahead. Cover and refrigerate.)*

FOR MOUSSE: Line 9 x 5 x 3-inch loaf pan with parchment paper. Combine Milky Way pieces, semisweet chocolate, unsweetened chocolate and 4 tablespoons unsalted butter in large heatproof bowl set over pan of simmering water. Stir constantly until melted (mixture will look grainy). Remove bowl from over water and cool mixture slightly.

Combine ½ cup sugar and water in heavy small saucepan. Stir over low heat until sugar dissolves. Increase heat to high and boil syrup until temperature reaches 230°F on candy thermometer. Meanwhile, beat egg whites and cream of tartar until soft peaks form.

Gradually pour boiling syrup into egg whites, beating until stiff peaks form and whites are cool, about 5 minutes. Using rubber spatula, fold whites into chocolate mixture in 2 additions. Beat 1¼ cups chilled whipping cream and 1 teaspoon vanilla extract to soft peaks in medium bowl. Using rubber spatula, fold cream into chocolate mixture in 2 additions. Spoon mousse into prepared pan. Cover with plastic wrap and freeze until firm, at least 6 hours. *(Can be prepared 1 week ahead. Keep frozen.)*

Heat sauce to lukewarm over low heat. Remove plastic wrap from top of mousse. Invert mousse onto platter. Remove pan and peel off parchment paper. Slice mousse crosswise into 12 slices. Cut each slice diagonally into 2 triangles. For each serving, arrange 2 mousse triangles on plate; spoon warm chocolate sauce over and around mousse and serve.

12 SERVINGS

◆ ◆ ◆

Remember the frozen Milky Way bars of your childhood? Here's a grown-up mousse to bring back those sweet memories.

◆ ◆ ◆

Frozen Raspberry Zabaglione on Meringues with Chocolate Sauce

◆ ◆ ◆

2   12-ounce bags frozen unsweetened raspberries, thawed, with juices
2   tablespoons corn syrup

8   large egg yolks
3/4 cup sugar
6   tablespoons Grand Marnier or other orange liqueur
5   tablespoons frozen orange juice concentrate, thawed

6   ounces bittersweet (not unsweetened) or semisweet chocolate, chopped
1   tablespoon light corn syrup
1   tablespoon water

3   large egg whites
1/4 teaspoon cream of tartar
3/4 cup sugar
1   cup sliced almonds, lightly toasted

FOR ZABAGLIONE: Puree raspberries and juices in blender. Strain puree into bowl, pressing hard on fruit to release all pulp and juices. Mix 2 tablespoons corn syrup into puree. Cover and refrigerate while preparing zabaglione.

Combine 8 egg yolks, 3/4 cup sugar, Grand Marnier and orange juice concentrate in large bowl. Using electric mixer, beat yolk mixture 1 minute. Set bowl over large saucepan of simmering water and beat yolk mixture at high speed until very thick and thermometer registers 160°F, about 12 minutes.

Place bowl over larger bowl filled with ice and water and cool zabaglione, whisking occasionally, about 15 minutes. Fold in 3/4 cup raspberry puree. Transfer to covered container and freeze. *(Can be prepared 2 days ahead.)*

FOR SAUCE: Stir chopped chocolate, 1 tablespoon corn syrup, 1 tablespoon water and 1/2 cup plus 3 tablespoons raspberry puree in heavy medium saucepan over low heat until chocolate melts and sauce is smooth. Cover and refrigerate. *(Can be made 2 days ahead.)*

FOR MERINGUES: Preheat oven to 200°F. Line large baking sheet with foil; grease foil lightly. Using electric mixer, beat 3 egg whites and 1/4 teaspoon cream of tartar in large bowl until soft peaks form.

◆ ◆ ◆

Zabaglione is the Italian version of the foamy, custardy sauce known as *sabayon* in France. Freezing it gives it a texture much like that of ice cream. For an extra-pretty presentation, garnish with fresh raspberries, orange segments, mint leaves and additional sliced, toasted almonds.

◆ ◆ ◆

Gradually add ¾ cup sugar, beating until meringue is stiff and shiny. Fold in half of toasted almonds.

Drop meringue in 8 mounds onto prepared sheet. Using back of spoon, make indentation in each mound. Sprinkle meringues with remaining toasted almonds. Bake 1 hour. Turn off oven, leave oven door closed and let meringues dry in oven overnight.

Place meringues on platter and fill each with large scoop of zabaglione. Wrap meringues and freeze at least 8 and up to 24 hours.

Rewarm chocolate sauce over low heat. Place each filled meringue on plate. Spoon warm chocolate sauce over.

8 SERVINGS

Frozen Chocolate Maple Roll
with Fudge Glaze

◆ ◆ ◆

1   cup pure maple syrup
⅛   teaspoon salt
2   large egg yolks
1   large egg

1½ cups chilled whipping cream

6   large eggs, separated, room temperature
¾   cup sugar
1   teaspoon vanilla extract
7   tablespoons unsweetened cocoa powder
¼   teaspoon cream of tartar

½   cup unsweetened cocoa powder
6   tablespoons whipping cream
½   cup pure maple syrup
2   tablespoons (¼ stick) unsalted butter

1   cup chopped toasted walnuts

FOR FILLING: Line bottom and sides of 17¼ x 11½-inch jelly roll pan with foil. Bring 1 cup syrup and salt to simmer in heavy medium saucepan. Beat yolks and 1 egg in medium bowl to blend. Gradually whisk hot syrup into egg mixture. Return mixture to saucepan. Stir constantly over medium heat until custard thickens and leaves path on back of spoon when finger is drawn across, about 4 minutes; do not boil. Pour mixture into large bowl. Set bowl in larger bowl filled with ice and water. Cool to room temperature, stirring occasionally, about 10 minutes.

Using electric mixer, beat 1½ cups cream in another bowl to stiff peaks. Fold ¼ of cream into egg mixture. Fold in remaining cream. Spread mixture in prepared pan; smooth top. Cover with plastic wrap and then freeze overnight.

FOR CAKE: Position rack in lowest third of oven and preheat to 350°F. Line another 17¼ x 11½-inch jelly roll pan with waxed paper, overlapping sides. Using electric mixer, beat yolks, ½ cup sugar and vanilla in large bowl until pale yellow and very thick, about 5 minutes. Sift 5 tablespoons cocoa over yolk mixture and fold together. Using electric mixer fitted with clean dry beaters, beat whites and cream of tartar in medium bowl until soft peaks form. Gradually add remaining ¼ cup sugar, beating until stiff but not dry. Fold ¼ of whites into yolk mixture to lighten. Fold in remaining whites. Pour batter into prepared pan; smooth top. Bake until toothpick inserted into center comes out clean, about 15 minutes. Cool cake completely in pan on rack.

Run small sharp knife around pan sides to loosen cake. Sift 2 tablespoons cocoa over large sheet of foil. Invert cake onto foil; peel off paper. Peel plastic off frozen filling. Invert filling atop cake. Peel off foil. Starting at 1 long side and using foil under cake as aid, roll up cake jelly roll style. Arrange cake seam side down on large platter. Freeze cake 1 hour.

FOR GLAZE: Place ½ cup cocoa in heavy small saucepan. Gradually whisk in 6 tablespoons cream, then ½ cup syrup. Bring mixture to boil, whisking constantly. Remove from heat. Add butter and whisk until melted. Cool to room temperature.

Spread glaze over frozen cake. Immediately press nuts onto top and sides of cake. Freeze until glaze sets, about 30 minutes. Cover with plastic and freeze cake until filling is firm, at least 8 hours or overnight. Slice cake and serve.

12 SERVINGS

Café Liégeois

◆ ◆ ◆

²⁄₃   *cup chilled crème fraîche or whipping cream*
1   *tablespoon sugar*
1   *tablespoon instant espresso powder or instant coffee powder*
1   *tablespoon coffee liqueur*
1   *pint vanilla ice cream, softened*

½   *cup chilled whipping cream*
1   *tablespoon sugar*
   Chocolate-covered coffee beans (optional)

FOR ICE CREAM: Beat chilled crème fraîche, 1 tablespoon sugar, instant espresso powder and coffee liqueur in medium bowl to stiff peaks. Add ice cream and fold together. Freeze overnight.

FOR TOPPING: Beat whipping cream and 1 tablespoon sugar in medium bowl to stiff peaks. Scoop ice cream into tall glasses. Garnish with dollop of whipped cream and top with coffee bean.

6 SERVINGS

◆ ◆ ◆

A delicious rendition of a classic
French and Belgian ice cream dessert.

Apple Butter Swirl Ice Cream Pie
with Maple Apples

◆ ◆ ◆

$^3/_4$ cup graham cracker crumbs
$^1/_2$ cup finely chopped walnuts
4   tablespoons ($^1/_2$ stick) unsalted butter, melted
2   tablespoons firmly packed golden brown sugar

$1^1/_2$ cups milk
$1^1/_2$ cups whipping cream
5   egg yolks
$^2/_3$ cup plus 2 tablespoons pure maple syrup

$^1/_4$ cup apple butter
1   tablespoon unsalted butter

$^1/_3$ cup chopped toasted walnuts

2   tablespoons ($^1/_4$ stick) unsalted butter
4   Red Delicious apples (about $1^3/_4$ pounds), peeled, cored, sliced
$^1/_4$ cup pure maple syrup

FOR CRUST: Preheat oven to 350°F. Combine first 4 ingredients in medium bowl, mixing well with fork. Press mixture onto bottom and up sides of 9-inch-diameter metal pie pan. Bake until set, about 15 minutes. Cool.

FOR ICE CREAM: Combine milk and 1 cup cream in heavy medium saucepan and bring to boil. Whisk egg yolks and $^2/_3$ cup maple syrup to blend in medium bowl. Gradually whisk in hot milk mixture. Return mixture to saucepan. Stir over medium-low heat until custard thickens and coats back of spoon, about 7 minutes; do not boil. Immediately whisk in remaining $^1/_2$ cup cream. Refrigerate custard until well chilled.

Bring apple butter and 2 tablespoons maple syrup to boil in heavy small saucepan. Remove from heat and whisk in 1 tablespoon butter. Set apple butter mixture aside.

Transfer custard to ice cream maker and process according to manufacturer's instructions. Spoon half of ice cream into prepared crust. Drizzle half of apple butter mixture over. Using small knife, swirl apple butter into ice cream. Repeat with remaining ice cream and apple butter. Sprinkle top with walnuts. Freeze overnight.

◆ ◆ ◆

To save time, purchased vanilla ice cream can be substituted for the maple ice cream in this treat.

◆ ◆ ◆

FOR APPLES: Melt 2 tablespoons butter in heavy large skillet over medium-high heat. Add apples and sauté until almost tender, about 7 minutes. Add ¼ cup maple syrup; stir until apples are tender and coated thickly with syrup, about 4 minutes.

Cut ice cream pie into wedges and serve with hot apples.

8 SERVINGS

Plum Raspberry Sorbet

◆ ◆ ◆

³/₄ cup plus 2 tablespoons sugar
²/₃ cup water

1¼ pounds plums, halved, pitted
2½ ½-pint baskets raspberries
¼ to 1 teaspoon fresh lemon juice
    Pinch of salt

    Fresh sliced plums
    Fresh raspberries
    Fresh mint sprigs

Stir sugar and water in heavy small saucepan over low heat until sugar dissolves. Increase heat to high; boil syrup 1 minute. Chill until cold, about 1 hour.

Puree 1¼ pounds plums and 2½ baskets raspberries in processor. Strain puree through fine sieve into medium bowl. Add syrup, lemon juice to taste and salt and blend well.

Process in ice cream machine according to manufacturer's instructions. Spoon sorbet into covered container and freeze. *(Can be prepared 2 days ahead.)*

Scoop sorbet into bowls. Garnish with plums, raspberries and mint sprigs and serve.

MAKES 4 CUPS

Snowdrop Brownies

♦ ♦ ♦

$^2/_3$ cups all purpose flour
$^1/_2$ cup unsweetened cocoa powder
$^1/_2$ teaspoon baking powder
$^1/_2$ teaspoon salt
1 cup sugar
$^1/_2$ cup (1 stick) unsalted butter, room temperature
2 eggs
1 teaspoon vanilla extract
$^1/_2$ cup white chocolate chips

Preheat oven to 350°F. Butter 8 x 8 x 2-inch glass baking dish. Sift first 4 ingredients into small bowl. Beat sugar, butter, eggs and vanilla together in medium bowl. Mix in dry ingredients. Mix in chips. Spread batter in prepared dish.

Bake until tester inserted into center comes out with moist crumbs still attached, about 25 minutes. Cool completely. Cut brownies into 2-inch squares.

MAKES 16

♦ ♦ ♦

The original campfire treat for kids gets dressed up for a grown-up party. Use a candy bar with a chocolate cream filling, like Lindt Chocolate Truffle. For nostalgia's sake, you can roast the marshmallows outdoors, but this dessert is just as good when done in the broiler.

♦ ♦ ♦

Chocolate Truffle S'mores

♦ ♦ ♦

12 wheat meal biscuits or graham cracker halves
2 3.5-ounce bittersweet chocolate candy bars, broken into segments
12 large marshmallows, cut in half

Preheat broiler. Arrange 6 biscuits on cookie sheet. Top with chocolate segments, then marshmallows, dividing evenly. Broil until marshmallows brown, watching closely. Cover with remaining biscuits, pressing gently. Serve hot.

6 SERVINGS

Lemon Shortbread

◆ ◆ ◆

1¼ cups all purpose flour

⅓ cup sugar

½ cup (1 stick) chilled unsalted butter, cut into pieces

1 tablespoon minced lemon peel

1 tablespoon fresh lemon juice

Powdered sugar

Preheat oven to 300°F. Grease large baking sheet. Sift flour and ⅓ cup sugar into large bowl. Add butter and lemon peel; rub with fingertips until mixture resembles coarse meal. Add lemon juice; press mixture with hands until dough holds together. Turn out dough onto lightly floured work surface. Divide dough in half. Gather each dough half into ball.

Place dough balls on prepared baking sheet, spacing evenly. Flatten each into 5½-inch round. Crimp edges decoratively with fingertips or fork. Using sharp knife, score 6 wedges into each round. Pierce surface all over with fork. Bake until light brown and firm to touch, about 50 minutes. Cut into wedges along scored lines. Cool 10 minutes. Sift powdered sugar over shortbreads on baking sheet. Transfer to rack; cool. *(Can be made 4 days ahead. Store in airtight container at room temperature.)*

MAKES 12

◆ ◆ ◆

Buttery shortbread with a touch of lemon is the perfect partner for a cup of steaming tea.

◆ ◆ ◆

Hazelnut and Anisette Biscotti

♦ ♦ ♦

2   cups all purpose flour
1   tablespoon grated lemon peel
1   tablespoon instant espresso powder or instant coffee powder
2 ½ teaspoons baking powder
2   teaspoons aniseed, finely chopped
1   teaspoon salt
½   cup (1 stick) chilled unsalted butter, cut into ½-inch pieces
1½ cups hazelnuts, toasted, husked (about 8½ ounces)
1   cup sugar
2   eggs
¼   cup anisette (anise-flavored liqueur)

Preheat oven to 350°F. Butter and flour 2 cookie sheets. Mix first 6 ingredients in processor. Add butter and cut in until mixture resembles coarse meal. Add nuts and sugar and chop nuts coarsely, using on/off turns. Transfer to large bowl. Mix eggs and anisette in small bowl. Add to dry ingredients and mix until dough forms.

Divide dough into 3 pieces. Gently knead each piece to bind. Form each into 1½-inch-wide log. Transfer to prepared sheets. Bake until golden brown and firm to touch, about 35 minutes. Cool in pans on racks 15 minutes.

Using serrated knife, cut logs into ¾-inch-thick slices. Arrange cut side up on cookie sheets. Bake until golden brown, about 15 minutes per side. Cool on rack. Store in airtight container.

MAKES ABOUT 48

Easy Fruit Pinwheels

♦ ♦ ♦

1   frozen puff pastry sheet, thawed (half of 17¼-ounce package)
½   cup sugar (about)
½   cup (about) jam or preserves

Preheat oven to 400°F. Roll out pastry sheet on work surface to remove creases. Brush pastry with water. Starting at 1 edge, roll up pastry tightly jelly roll style. Cut pastry into generous ¼-inch-thick rounds. Place sugar on plate and press 1 round into sugar. Set round on baking sheet, sugar side up, tucking end under. Repeat with

♦ ♦ ♦

Apricot and berry jams are especially nice in these quick cookies.

remaining pastry rounds. Press center of each round with finger to form small hollow. Spoon 1 teaspoon jam into each hollow. Sprinkle pastries with additional sugar.

Bake pastries until golden brown, about 20 minutes. Cool on racks. *(Can be prepared 6 hours ahead.)*

MAKES ABOUT 24

Pine Nut Caramel Bars

◆ ◆ ◆

$^3/_4$ cup *(1$^1/_2$ sticks) unsalted butter, room temperature*
$^1/_3$ *cup sugar*
2 $^1/_4$ *teaspoons grated lemon peel*
1 $^1/_2$ *cups all purpose flour*
$^1/_4$ *cup cornstarch*
$^1/_4$ *teaspoon salt*

6   *tablespoons ($^3/_4$ stick) unsalted butter*
6   *tablespoons firmly packed dark brown sugar*
$^1/_4$ *cup honey*
1 $^3/_4$ *cups pine nuts (about 8 $^1/_2$ ounces)*
1 $^1/_2$ *tablespoons whipping cream*

FOR PASTRY: Preheat oven to 350°F. Line 8-inch square glass baking dish with foil. Using electric mixer, beat $^3/_4$ cup butter in large bowl until light. Add $^1/_3$ cup sugar and lemon peel and beat until light and fluffy. Mix flour, cornstarch and salt in small bowl. Add to butter mixture and mix until beginning to gather together. Press dough over bottom and 1 inch up sides of prepared dish. Pierce dough all over with fork. Bake until beginning to color, about 35 minutes. Remove crust from oven; maintain oven temperature.

FOR TOPPING: Combine butter, packed dark bown sugar and honey in heavy medium saucepan. Whisk over medium-high heat until mixture comes to boil. Boil without whisking until mixture thickens and bubbles enlarge, about 1 minute. Stir in pine nuts. Remove from heat; stir in whipping cream.

Spread topping in crust. Bake until caramel bubbles, about 20 minutes. Cool completely in pan on rack. Remove from pan, using foil as aid. Cut into squares. *(Can be prepared 2 days ahead. Store in airtight container.)*

MAKES 16

Gingersnap Cannoli with Dried Cherry Filling

◆ ◆ ◆

2 tablespoons sugar
2 tablespoons unsalted butter
2 tablespoons dark corn syrup
³/₄ teaspoon ground ginger
¹/₄ teaspoon fresh lemon juice
¹/₄ cup all purpose flour
1 1¹/₄-inch-thick wooden dowel or cannoli form

3 tablespoons sugar
2 tablespoons bourbon
2 tablespoons dried currants
2 tablespoons chopped dried Bing cherries or golden raisins
2 teaspoons grated orange peel (orange part only)

³/₄ cup mascarpone cheese*
1¹/₂ teaspoons Grand Marnier or other orange liqueur
¹/₄ cup chilled whipping cream

3 tablespoons chopped toasted pistachios
Powdered sugar

FOR CANNOLI: Preheat oven to 375°F. Combine first 5 ingredients in small saucepan. Stir over low heat until sugar dissolves and butter melts. Remove from heat. Add flour 1 tablespoon at a time,

stirring until smooth. Place 1 tablespoon dough on heavy nonstick cookie sheet. Using moistened fingertips, press dough to 4-inch round. Bake until cookie is crisp and darkens in color, about 10 minutes. Remove from oven. Let stand 30 seconds. Using flat metal spatula, loosen cookie from sheet. Immediately wrap around dowel, forming tube shape. Cool. Remove from dowel. Repeat with dough in 3 more batches. Store airtight in cool dry place up to 6 hours.

FOR FILLING: Combine 3 tablespoons sugar and next 4 ingredients in small skillet. Stir over low heat until sugar dissolves. Cook until almost all liquid is gone, about 4 minutes. Cool.

Combine fruit mixture and mascarpone in bowl. Mix in liqueur. Beat cream into stiff peaks. Fold into mascarpone. Chill 30 minutes.

Spoon filling into pastry bag fitted with ½-inch plain tip. Pipe filling into each cannoli. Dip ends in chopped nuts; dust with sugar.

*Available at Italian markets and some specialty foods stores.

MAKES 4

Nutty Chocolate Chip Cookies

◆ ◆ ◆

1   cup (2 sticks) unsalted butter, room temperature
¾   cup sugar
¾   cup firmly packed golden brown sugar
1   tablespoon vanilla extract
1   tablespoon Frangelico (hazelnut liqueur)
1   tablespoon coffee liqueur
2   large eggs
2½ cups all purpose flour
1   teaspoon baking soda
½   teaspoon salt
2   11½-ounce packages milk chocolate chips
1   cup chopped walnuts
½   cup chopped pecans
½   cup chopped macadamia nuts

Preheat oven to 325°F. Using electric mixer, beat first 6 ingredients in large bowl until light and fluffy. Add eggs and beat well. Mix flour, baking soda and salt in small bowl. Stir into butter mixture. Mix in chocolate chips and all chopped nuts. Drop batter by ¼ cupfuls onto ungreased cookie sheets, spacing apart. Bake until golden brown, about 16 minutes. Cool on racks.

MAKES ABOUT 3 DOZEN

PLAYFUL PARTY FAVORS FOR CHILDREN

When setting the table for a child's birthday party, let your imagination go, mixing colors of napkins, tablecloth, glasses and such and decorating with ribbons, bows and balloons. And when it comes to party favors, opt for toys kids can really play with. Here are some ideas:

◆ Decorate gift bags with stickers and fill with an assortment of Tinkertoy pieces, which appeal to children of almost every age.

◆ For kids over five, fill small net bags with an assortment of marbles, and include instructions for how to play.

◆ Take plain party bags and fill with a few rubber stamps, a pad of paper and several colored inks. Let the kids decorate their bags.

◆ ◆ ◆

•Index•

Strawberry Cheesecake in Macaroon Crust, page 186.

Acknowledgments

◆ ◆ ◆

The following people and restaurants contributed the recipes included in this book: All Seasons Cafe & Wine Shop, Calistoga, California; Ann FitzGerald's Farmhouse Kitchen, Mathry, Wales; David Badal; David Barash; Melanie Barnard; Mary Bergin; Lena Cederham Birnbaum; Lynn Black; The Black Tulip, Cocoa Village, Florida; Bonaventure Resort & Spa, Fort Lauderdale, Florida; Botafumeiro, Barcelona, Spain; The Boulders, Carefree, Arizona; Roxanne E. Chan; Chez Panisse, Berkeley, California; The Churchill House Inn, Brandon, Vermont; Clipper Cruise Line's World Discoverer; Courtney's Bistro, Caernarvon, Wales; Lane Crowther; Brooke Dojny; El Cholo, Los Angeles, California; Sue Ellison; Crystal Ettridge; Carine Fabius; Jim Fobel; Jill Foster; Jean Garry; Pascal Giacomini; Lina Gillies; Robin Levy Goetz; Rick and Carol Goings; The Golden Lemon Inn & Villas, Dieppe Bay, St. Kitts, West Indies; Heathcote's, Longridge, Lancashire, England; John and Elizabeth Galt Hirsch; Karen Kaplan; Lynne Rossetto Kasper; Kathleen's Grand Wailea Resort Hotel & Spa, Maui, Hawaii; Jeanne Thiel Kelley; Kristine Kidd; Charles and Jacqueline Kilvert; Elinor Klivans; La Table du Manoir, Hovey Manor, North Hatley, Quebec, Canada; L'Auberge du Père Bise, Lac d'Annecy, Talloires, France; Paul and Mary Lamontagne; Lancellotti Dining Room, Geneva On The Lake, Geneva, New York; Teresa Lawrence; Le Chêne Madame, Neuville-en-Condroz, Belgium; Jim Lingenfelter; The Lodge at Pebble Beach, Pebble Beach, California; Louise's Trattoria, Los Angeles, California; Emily Luchetti; Michael McLaughlin; Alice Medrich; Eric and Lee Miller; Moosewood Restaurant, Ithaca, New York; Selma Brown Morrow; A Pacific Cafe, Kauai, Hawaii; Palace Court, Caesars Palace, Las Vegas, Nevada; Park Bistro, New York, New York; Piemonte Ovest, Oakland, California; Rebecca Poynor-Burns; Steven Raichlen; Betty Rosbottom; Cynthia Rowley; The Ryland Inn, Whitehouse, New Jersey; Julie Sahni; Patricia Cohen Samuels; Sanford Restaurant, Milwaukee, Wisconsin; Richard Sax; Carole Schreder; Shana Schuman; Showley's at Miramonte, St. Helena, California; Marie Simmons; Eileen Smith; Tom Sullivan; Todd Taverner; Sarah Tenaglia; Shula Udoff; Joanne Weir; White Moss House, Grasmere, Cumbria, England.

The following people contributed the photographs included in this book: Jack Andersen; Caroline Arber; Asian Art & Archaeology/Art Resource; Rick Beattie; David Bishop; Cynthia Brown; Michael Bryant; Ric Cohn; Wyatt Counts; Katrina De Leon; Deborah Denker; Julie Dennis; Michael Deuson; Jody Dole; Alison Duke; Mark Ferri; Tony Giammarino; Michael Grand; Henry Hamamoto; Jim Hansen; Michael Lamotte; Brian Leatart; Leong Ka Tai; Breeze Munson; Gabriela Ortuzar; Jan Oswald; Diane Padys; Kathlene Persoff; Judd Pilossof; Steven Rothfeld; Jeremy Samuelson; Jeff Sarpa; Bruce Van Inwegen; Francine Zaslow.

Front Jacket Photo: Cynthia Brown, Photographer; Georgia Downard, Food Stylist; Jeannie Oberholtzer, Stylist. Footed cake plate from the *Alice Collection*, Orrefors, 140 Bradford Drive, Berlin, NJ 08009.